Finding Leadership

Building Teams
That Build Your Business

Kristen McAlister

ISBN-13: 978-1-7335026-5-8

CERIUS EXECUTIVES 100 SPECTRUM CENTER DRIVE SUITE 900 IRVINE CA 92618

www.ceriusexecutives.com

Table of Contents

Preface 5

Section 1: GETTING OUT OF THE WEEDS.......................... 7

Journey of a Founder/CEO 7

Stuck in the Weeds... 10

What Does Being in the Weeds Look Like?.............. 14

What Should the Founder's Role Be?........................17

Section 2: BUILDING LEADERSHIP TEAMS THAT BUILD A

BUSINESS 30

Where Are You Taking the Company? 37

What Do You Need Done? 43

Whom Do You Need to Do It?................................... 49

Section 3: GROWTH STRATEGIES: COMPANY AND

EMPLOYEES 59

Setting Expectations...62

Developing Leadership 67

When One Outgrows the Other.................................76

Section 4: LEADERSHIP TEAM ALIGNMENT **90**

Getting Aligned 91

Clarity 93

Consistency 94

Communication 96

Collaboration 100

Conflict 102

Culture 103

Section 5: GET FORWARD MOVEMENT **107**

Remove the Roadblocks 108

Comfort Zones 113

Let Your Leadership Team Lead 115

Epilogue: This Founder's Journey 119

Final Thought: Your Journey 123

Acknowledgements 124

About the Author 125

Preface

We all start companies for different reasons. Sometimes we are inspired by an idea we can't believe no one else has thought of before. Other times, it's the desire to do our own thing, to never have a boss again. Whatever the reason, founders pour their blood, sweat, and tears into their companies. Overall, it's worth it ... most days, well, some days.

It's always fun in the beginning. The new, the exciting, the fast-paced nature of it all. Then one day it happens: We succeed. We have employees and customers and vendors and taxes. We end up being the person who answers every question. Settles every dispute. Creates every plan. At this point, it stops being fun. Our title says founder, owner, president, CEO, but honestly, we feel like an underappreciated project manager. One who reports to everyone — the employees, the customers, the vendors, the tax man — only to have nowhere to turn when we run out of answers.

This journey describes thousands of company leaders today. Maybe you are one of them. Maybe you are one of the employees experiencing this alongside the owner. Our success has trapped us. It has taken that great idea we started with, that desire for the freedom for which we risked everything, and it has turned those things upside down — and sometimes against us. Our passion for the idea may be fading, along with our freedom. And that's been gone for years. When was the last time we took a vacation, let alone an uninterrupted vacation? We care about our companies, and everyone connected to them, but it wasn't supposed to be like this; it wasn't supposed to be this hard.

The good news is you're right: It isn't supposed to be like this, and it doesn't have to be this hard. There is a solution. In this book, we will talk through a problem you are mostly all too familiar with, then walk together through a solution that can give you back the company you started. It won't be easy — you are going to have to address some really hard questions and make some even harder decisions — but it's for your own good. This journey will give you your company back. More importantly, it will give you your life back.

Any one of us could be the individual in any of the examples. While the stories and journeys of the leaders in this book are inspired by real events (used with permission), this work is ultimately a work of fiction, using fictionalized characters to allow the reader the opportunity to better relate to the concepts in the book.

CHAPTER 1

Journey of a Founder/CEO

Imagine a commercial food manufacturing plant. Everyone is focused on what they are doing, from processing the food to making sure the temperature and timing is right in 50-gallon vats of soups and sauces. Next thing you know, there's smoke coming out of the laundry room, and the commercial dryer is on fire. Unknown to anyone at this moment, the lint trap has caught fire. That's what happens when it doesn't get cleaned out regularly. The wet clothes are in the drum. When they get dry enough, they heat up. The lint becomes kindling, goes through the flue, and passes through the flames; the fire rolls back through the flue, and the contents in the drying drum go up in flames.

What would you do? It is a contained fire. You can see it rolling in the drum round and round — it's quite hypnotic. It is easy enough to think through what to do in that situation and what the various options are. You can turn off the machine, but there is still enough oxygen for the fire to stay ignited. Inclination is to wait for the fire department. Another option is to grab a fire extinguisher to put out the flames; just prepare for the hot surfaces you are about to touch. There are ways to mitigate the risk. It would be over in 20 seconds. Either way, there are options.

In this particular situation, the owner of the company, Carrie, was at another location when the fire started. An employee called to tell her there was a fire. Carrie couldn't do anything. Fifteen minutes away, she was useless to them. She said, "Put it out; I'll be right there." She ran to her car and drove 7 miles in 7 minutes. What did she find when she got there? The dryer was still on, drum still rotating, contents still burning. She grabbed any number of heat-resistant items they used to handle the 50-gallon vats, wrapped her arms, lined up people with fire extinguishers, and within a few minutes, the fire was out. Those who helped put the fire out were the same individuals who were there when the fire started.

Why did they wait for Carrie to arrive to put out the fire? The response: "You didn't tell us how to put out the fire, so we waited for you."

It had not occurred to Carrie that she needed to put an SOP (standard operating procedure) in place to cover putting out a contained fire. She felt she had failed as a leader in not empowering her employees to solve problems themselves. She was blown away that this happened on her watch. They didn't put the fire out. They didn't call the fire department. They called her to come put out the fire.

The following weekend, Carrie met up with a longtime friend, Ron, and told him what had happened. "In hindsight, it was my fault; I allowed this to happen," she said. "I should have been there, or I should have trained the team on how to put out a fire. I'll add that to our monthly safety briefing."

Ron could see and hear Carrie's pain and frustration. He knew she had been working long hours, and she couldn't see a clear path ahead. Now she was talking through what else she needed to add to her plate because of the fire.

He told her an SOP would not have mattered. He talked about the need to empower and trust her team to solve a problem without her there and without an SOP. This was not the first time they'd had a discussion like this. Ron knew it was time to introduce her to someone who could really help.

Willie is a CEO coach and facilitator. He runs a group of leaders that gets together monthly to talk about their businesses, struggles, and successes. It might be good for Carrie to learn from others who have been in similar situations and find out how they are growing their companies. Ron could see Carrie was stuck in the weeds of her business, and he knew she needed to hear from others beyond him to get out of them.

CHAPTER 2

Stuck in the Weeds

Carrie was open to meeting Willie. They got together at one of her favorite restaurants for lunch the following Wednesday. Carrie wasn't the best with change and trying something new, so she found comfort in meeting somewhere familiar.

For the second time in a week, Carrie retold her story about the fire. Each time she told it, the fire got bigger, and her self-esteem got smaller.

Willie listened and seemed to hang on every word. He was very personable and started off by reassuring Carrie that she wasn't alone. Though hers was the first story involving an actual fire, he had heard many versions through the years. These included the loss of a big customer and needing to make up 30% of the business, as well as needing to figure out how to grow 15% next year. One owner, all of a sudden, had their marketing leads drop by 50% overnight; another had a key member of the team quit with no notice. Things happen that seemingly threaten the health and safety of the company and the team.

The journey of being a founder, owner, and/or CEO is a roller coaster. There are many models, articles, and books available about the various stages a company goes through as it grows (or doesn't grow). Willie shared what he traditionally saw as a founder's journey when starting and growing a company. As a business owner who had already grown one business and currently owned a second, Willie knew this journey firsthand.

Early on, the business requires a lot of Swiss Army knives, a.k.a. generalists. The CEO is creating the product/service, growing the customer base, managing (and likely doing) the accounting, and managing the product creation or service delivery. As it grows, we add in administrative support and others to help get tasks done. As owners, we remain a one-person leadership team. Everyone who works with us is doing multiple roles with the goal of simply getting the task done. This is the period of time when we introduce ourselves as "chief toilet scrubber" rather than CEO.

The company continues to grow, and we need to take some things off our plate. We start to offload either the tasks we don't like doing or the tasks that are easy to transfer. Our administrative support is now the office manager, who helps with hiring, onboarding, and managing. They have never managed anyone before, but they know where everything is and how it should be done. The office manager starts helping with accounting, project management, and anything else they are willing to take off our plates. Eventually, other parts of the business need help, and we dedicate more resources to them. The office manager moves into operations or accounting. They continue growing in responsibilities, changing their title to controller (or, better yet, CFO) or director of operations. We likely have a great culture of teamwork with everyone pitching in where needed. All is good.

Then we hit a wall. That wall is built by some area of struggle. It could be slowed sales growth or operational issues. We're spending too much to deliver our product/service, we start losing team members, and we have never worked so hard to make so little money. We keep trying ideas that make little to no difference. The two people we rely on most are doing what they should be doing. They were two of the first hires we made. They are reliable, they get things done, and we can't imagine what it would be like without them. If we could just figure out how to solve the issues of sales, operations, etc., things would get better. In our minds, the reason things aren't working the way they should is our team is overworked and taking on way too much. We can hire more people to help them. If we get them more help and more time to train and document, we can stop making mistakes, and growth will be easier. The team is looking to us, the CEO, for the solution.

As Willie described this situation, Carrie related to it. She had come up with the idea for her business. She started helping friends commercialize their recipes to sell food to local markets. She now has a 50,000-square-foot facility producing 5,000 gallons of food per day. Every process, every product/service, every part of the business has her thumbprint on it. Of course, no one does it better than she does it. She created it. And since no one does it better, she should be the one to do it. She believes that if it isn't done her way, it won't get done correctly, and she'll then need to jump in and fix it. Of course, she could spend a couple of years and hundreds of thousands of dollars finding someone else to do it exactly like she does. Carrie didn't see the point of going through all that.

As Carrie shared her thoughts with Willie, it was easy for him to see what was going on with her company. Willie is familiar with this thought process. He was able to easily recognize when a founder was stuck in the weeds. Carrie reminded him of one of his CEO group members, Max, who had left the group last year. At one point, Max had engaged an M&A firm to value his business and help him sell it. Max's company distributed ethnic products to specialty supermarkets. Much of it was from Mexico, both perishable and shelf stable. Max was at a $15 million–$20 million run rate with revenue when he decided to try to sell his company.

Unfortunately, the M&A firm pointed out a big obstacle to selling it: Max. He was the person who goes to the tractor trailer and looks at the shipment of bananas to determine if they are ripe enough. He hires/fires, and he does the QuickBooks accounting work, customer contracts, and day-to-day inspections. He communicates bilingually with the team, the vendors, and the customers. He decides what they accept or reject from their vendors, and he does this Monday–Saturday. When a shipment arrives, he can be found at the truck. The M&A advisor tried to help Max identify any elements of what he did that could be done by someone else and hire people for those responsibilities. They struggled to find someone to replace any of Max's responsibilities. The advisor sent him three resumés of people who do similar things, but Max saw his own skill set as unique. No one else is familiar enough with the various items coming in on the truck. Max understands the culture, the foods, the quality, etc. None of the candidates understood his culture, his specific food products, the exact quality he was looking for. While there are many companies doing the same or similar things as his company, and most people coming from those companies could be trained, Max believed he had to be the one to do everything. He eventually left the group, because his business continued to grow, and he couldn't be away from it one day a month.

CHAPTER 3

What Does Being in the Weeds Look Like?

As Willie told this story to Carrie, her head dropped. She stared into her salad before looking back up at Willie. He could see he was on the right track and asked her a few additional questions:

1. Do you lead every meeting in the company?
2. Do you already have the answer in your head when you ask your team a question?
3. Do you use weekends for catching up on work rather than doing something for yourself or spending time with friends and family?

He knew the answers without waiting for a response.

Just because we *can* do something doesn't mean we *should* do something. It is likely true that no one can do it better than Max — or Carrie — can do it. This is based on the assumption that the only way to do things is Max's way. Willie continued to point out the fallacy in Max's rationale.

Sometimes we confuse *how* we do things for *why* we do things. One is process driven, and one is culture driven. Max's role should be setting the why we do what we do. That provides guidelines for everyone to figure out how to do it. As the company evolves, the how needs to evolve with the company. That isn't always true for culture, which should remain constant and be the thread woven through everything the company does.

There is a reason so many business owners get caught in the weeds. It is often easier for people to be the firefighter than the fire chief. Willie knew this would resonate with Carrie. It is hard giving up product decisions on a product we created. It is tough not knowing how everything in the company is done and needing to ask someone in accounting for a finance report rather than pulling it ourselves. It is tough asking someone to make a correction that would take us less time to correct ourselves. When we do try to hire someone, we want everything to be done the exact same way we do it. Unfortunately, this is often an uphill battle with training that ends up in frustration. We are trying to find someone exactly like us.

Willie decided to use an example that Carrie could easily relate to. When the founder is growing the business, it is like a client asking you to recreate a recipe their grandmother used to make. There is no recipe and no finished product to sample. They are recalling ingredients that were sitting on her counter and how good it tasted. They can't recall what it tasted like, but it was the best sauce they had ever tasted. There is no clarity for what you need to make for them, other than the best version of that food that ever existed.

Willie suggested Carrie come visit his next meeting in two weeks. It would give her a chance to meet some of the other leaders and get an idea of what it is like to be a member of the group. Carrie started giving him every reason why she couldn't take a couple of hours away from the office to join. Willie then asked a question Carrie would never forget: "How much more of your current situation are you willing to endure and for how much longer?" She thought about what the past couple of years had been like and agreed to come check out the meeting.

CHAPTER 4

What Should the Founder's Role Be?

Two weeks later, Carrie showed up to an industrial park at 7:45 am. She had no idea what to expect. She made her way through the front door, followed the signs to the meeting, and was able to hear the group before she walked into the room. She saw a group of individuals, dressed casually, grabbing some breakfast and coffee. They eventually all sat down at a U-shaped table. Carrie did a scan of the table and the tent cards in front of each person with their name and company name. A few of the company names she recognized, but most she had never heard of before. She had no idea what she had gotten herself into.

To start the meeting, Willie had each person introduce themselves. Carrie was intrigued listening to information about each company, the individual's role in the company, and the top challenge they were facing. Some posed a question to the group for input at some point during the day. As the members gave their title and role, a few stood out to her.

Evette was the CEO, not the owner, of a truck maintenance company. Carrie found it interesting that Evette didn't own the company. As Carrie got to know Evette throughout the day, she learned quite a bit. The current owner had bought it from the founder a few years ago. The business had been doing about $2 million–$3 million in revenue at that time. The former owner ran it as a founder/CEO, was stuck in the weeds, and decided to sell rather than grow the company. The new owner replaced the founder (who was more than happy to be replaced) and immediately recruited Evette to be the CEO. On the surface, it was easy to question this decision. She had no experience in trucking, maintenance, service, or distribution, and she would be leading a male-dominated company in a male-dominated industry. Her background also made it look like she was way overqualified for the job, given the size and revenues of companies she had worked for previously. The new owner was looking to grow, and he knew Evette would be driven to grow it, given her background and what she wanted out of her next role. She wanted to be CEO of a multilocation operation with the goal of being the one to expand it nationally.

Evette shared that they have had a firm aggressively trying to acquire them. But the new owner's ability to rely on someone else to run the business meant he was not as motivated as most to sell. Even if Evette decided to take another role, she has built a great team and knows the owner could easily put in a new CEO. He knows he has something stable and of value. He has stuck his ground on the negotiations, and the buyer has been the only one to move. It's an ideal situation for any owner: an outstanding CEO with a leadership team and management under them. This owner lives in Florida and visits the business a couple of times a year and collects the checks. He'd bought the company to grow it to the point where it would pay dividends. He started with getting the right CEO, Evette, who then built the team.

Carrie was intrigued by the fact that the new owner did not have the CEO title, nor was he involved in the business on a day-to-day basis. He acted more like an investor. He put the right leadership in place and let them run the daily operations of the company. Something has to go very wrong for the owner to get called in to assist. Carrie thought, "If a fire broke out, he would hear about it once the fire was put out, and everyone was out safely and accounted for." She was a bit jealous.

Another member, Bruce, had been a member of the group for more than 20 years. He had founded, grown, and sold a medical device company, and he was now an angel investor in a couple of companies.

There was also the president of a large construction company, Rich. Rich wasn't the founder or the CEO. He was the president. He had been with the company for more than 30 years, having started as a project manager in his early 20s. He had been promoted up through the company. Once he became an executive, he joined a leadership peer group made up of other leaders from various companies and disciplines. The company had invested a lot in him through the years to help him be ready for each promotion he accepted. He just moved into this group, since the CEO is looking at retiring in the next two years and wants Rich ready to step in as CEO at that time.

One of the newest members, Trevor, was part owner of a family-owned business. His dad started the business and had since stepped away from running it to focus entirely on sales. The reality was that his dad didn't like leading and managing, but he loved working with the customers. Trevor was struggling with what to call himself. His team was telling him he should be introducing himself as CEO, but he was more comfortable with a general manager or president title.

Another member of the group, Logan, gave a good distinction between the two. The president, or in Trevor's case, general manager, since he seemed comfortable with that title, is running the day-to-day, making sure the company has revenue coming in the door and profitability at the end of the day. The CEO is determining the direction of the company, getting rid of bottlenecks, and making sure the company has the resources to grow. Logan asked Trevor, "Are you focused on the daily profitability or the direction of the company?" Trevor knew the answer as soon as Logan asked the question. He sheepishly answered, "I'll start calling myself CEO."

Listening to the variety of people in the room and the explanation of a CEO vs. a president or general manager, Carrie wanted to get it all straight in her head. As nervous as she was about asking a question, she didn't have much to lose by asking: "It seems like a lot of titles for roles that are very similar and can be done by the same person. I'm comparing it with what I do every day, and I'm not clear on the nuances between some of the titles you just mentioned."

Willie was happy to help provide some clarity. Since so many owners play multiple roles in the company, it was helpful to give a few differences between them.

Investor

- Set the investment thesis: How is the company going to grow and give a return on investment?
- Monitor the progress of the investment.

CEO

- Be the "visionary." Set the vision for the company. Provide the picture of the destination, not necessarily the step-by-step directions on how to get there.
- Give clarity.
- Remove roadblocks.

President

- Full P&L responsibility: How are we going to make our goals?
- As the "integrator," manage the daily operations of the business.

Willie added some additional titles, namely chief financial officer (CFO) and chief operating officer (COO).

Chief Financial Officer

- Responsible for the financial health of the company.
- Analyze what has happened and its impact to the company, and provide insights for investor/owner decision making.
- Provide future scenarios for revenue and profitability.

Chief Operating Officer

- Responsible for revenue generation (not revenue via sales invoice, but revenue when the product is shipped or service is delivered) and for company profitability, based on what they are given responsibility for and visibility to.

Willie could see the confusion on Carrie's face as he talked through the chief operating officer, so he added: "Whether it is a product or a service company, and regardless of what method is used to recognize revenue, the opportunity for actual revenue is created by the sales team or sales individuals. The revenue and opportunity for profitability doesn't exist until the product or service is delivered. That is the responsibility of the operations leader.

"It makes sense early on for the founder to take on all these responsibilities, when all available cash should be put into the product and getting sales. As the company grows, and there's cash flow, the decisions and directions grow in complexity. There are different skill sets and perspectives to be an investor, a CEO, a president, and so on. As a company grows, it may be in the company's best interest to start separating these responsibilities."

Willie paused to make sure his explanation was connecting with Carrie. Bruce, the CEO turned angel investor, added: "We don't start, buy, or inherit a business with a dream to work 60-hour weeks, never taking a vacation, having our lives revolve around the company, and waking up every morning dreading what we will have to deal with today. Regardless of how much money we are or are not making at any given time, this is not the life most of us saw for ourselves. This is what happens when an owner is running the business rather than setting the destination and removing the obstacles."

Willie could see the morning coffee wearing off and called for a 15-minute break. He took Carrie aside and asked if she was comfortable sharing with the group about her background and situation. She took a deep breath and agreed.

After the break, it was Carrie's turn. She gave some background on why she started the company and what led to her being introduced to Willie. She said she honestly wasn't sure what she was looking for at this point but was open to figuring it out. This time it was Trevor who asked the question, "What role do you want in the company?" Her response was: "I'm not sure. I have been doing so much of the work for so long, I'm not sure what I want to do, and I don't see how I can trust anyone else to do most of what I do."

Carrie scanned the room. She clearly had hit a hot button, since everyone's hands were raised, and they were arguing about who was going to interject first. Rather than peppering her with questions or comments, Willie looked at the group. He knew each of their stories and the journeys they had all gone through. Most were very similar to Carrie's. Willie turned toward Logan, who had grown his company and recently brought in a president to run the business. He said, "Logan, why don't you share what you did to figure out what your role should be."

As Carrie listened to Logan give a little background on starting his company, she could see the similarities. Logan had built every piece of the company, including the technology behind his product and the web platform for his customers. Unfortunately, since he was capable of doing so many things, he did them. The path of least resistance was to do it himself. It got to the point that nothing happened in his company without his involvement. This resulted in 70-hour work weeks, not spending much time with his children, and never taking a vacation.

Logan hit a breaking point one day after an all-nighter and decided to get some help. The group had been suggesting for months that he bring in someone to help him. Logan was hesitant, since he'd had a couple of bad hires the past year and wasn't up for going through it again. One of the members in the group had worked with an interim operations leader a few years back and suggested Logan give him a call, which he did.

It took a few months and a lot of "two steps forward, three steps back," but Logan was able to see progress. One of the first exercises the interim leader walked him through was figuring out what Logan should continue to do and what responsibilities he needed to hand over to either the interim, someone else in the company, or a new hire. It took Logan some time to think through everything he did in the company. At first, he started to list every task in the company. He then started to see patterns with the tasks and found that multiple tasks fell into categories, such as "repetitive tasks" or "new things I get to explore." Though he was good at the repetitive tasks, they felt torturous to him. He did not like doing the same thing over and over, week after week. What really drove Logan and got him excited to wake up every morning was similar to why he started the company: He likes trying new ways to make the complicated simple and doing things no one else was thinking of yet.

Once Logan had listed out the tasks and grouped them into categories that made sense to him, the interim operations leader asked Logan to separate them into the following:

- What do I love doing and I am great at?
- What do I like doing and I am good at?
- What do I not like doing and I am good at?
- What do I not like doing and I am not good at?

They worked together to identify individuals in the company who could take on some of the responsibilities, who could be developed to do them, and who they needed to hire. This included a timeline for hiring someone to eventually replace the ongoing responsibilities of the interim operations leader.

It was not quick, and it was not easy, but eventually, Logan was able to take an uninterrupted vacation, work a normal work week, and get more time to work on the next generation of products and services. He loved being forward looking, speaking at industry conferences, and solving problems the industry didn't realize they had. He focused his efforts on the activities he loved doing and was great at.

By this point, Carrie's head was spinning. The group sensed this and knew that look. It was the same look each of them had on their first day visiting the meeting. Willie left her with the following: "If you are serious about growing your company without you being at the center of it, this group can help you. We are going to challenge you and frustrate you every step of the way."

The first three questions he said they were going to help her answer were:

1.   What is your role?

Think through the value you bring to the company that few others could bring. What is the highest and best use of your time to the company? What activities will benefit the company most by having you do them?

2. Where are you taking the company?

For now, this sets the foundation for everything else. It can be easily argued that this is determined before your role is decided. You may decide the company needs to double revenue in the next five years through acquisition. Based on your skills and experience, you may decide it makes sense to bring in a seasoned CEO with M&A experience. You'd step into the investor role and focus on initiatives that fit what you are great at and love to do. You may love the idea of M&A, but having not done it before, there are elements that make more sense for an experienced leader with prior experience to handle. There are many components to growing through acquisition, which include: integration of other companies into yours, making the tough decisions of who remains with the company and who doesn't, knowing what roadblocks to move and where, and communicating and messaging to all employees (current and new). Many of us enjoy the components of the M&A process, but few of us have the experience and expertise to manage all the components. If this is the strategy, think about what is best for the company. Is the owner the best person to be leading it, or is someone else?

3. Do you have the team to get there?

This is the million-dollar question everyone in the group struggles with continually. Once you decide the direction you want the company to go, the group will help you figure out what and who you need to get there. This includes evaluating who you have, getting alignment among your leadership team, and getting forward movement toward the outcome you want.

Smiling, they all wished Carrie well as she departed, and they continued the rest of their session. When Willie called her the next day to see what she thought about the meeting and if she was interested in joining the group, he chuckled at her response of, "Do I have a choice?"

She knew this was going to be uncomfortable. Carrie was used to being in control of every part of her company and her life. Not knowing the outcome and the exact path to get there is far outside her comfort zone. As much as she didn't like being constantly challenged, and the concept of being vulnerable gave her some anxiety, she knew she was going to need to address some difficult questions and make some decisions she had been putting off for far too long.

Pulling It All Together

Things to Know

- When a company is started, the founder takes on all leadership roles in the company and more.
- As the company grows, the responsibilities of the founder will widen in impact and decrease in quantity.
- The owner or CEO is most valuable when focusing on the highest and best use of their time and the responsibilities they enjoy.

Questions to Ask

- Does my team solve most problems that occur and work through lasting solutions for them, leaving me to focus on what I enjoy doing?
- Is the majority of my time spent on activities that provide the company with the most value?
- Am I happy and enjoying the role(s) and responsibilities I take on in the company?

Exercise

For clarity on your role and responsibilities in the company.

- List your current responsibilities. Categorize them if it helps.

- Separate the responsibilities into the following additional categories:
  - What do I love doing and I am great at?
  - What do I like doing and I am good at?
  - What do I not like doing and I am good at?
  - What do I not like doing and I am not good at?
- Decide which of the current responsibilities you will keep, which you will hand off.
  - To whom will you hand it off?
  - Who needs to be trained and developed to take on the responsibilities?
  - Which responsibilities will need an owner who is not in the company yet?
- Step back, and look at what you are keeping and which role best describes them.

Next Step: Taking Action

Be clear about your role and responsibilities in the company to help it grow, so it can be easily explained to a group of advisors and/or your internal team.

Section 2: BUILDING LEADERSHIP TEAMS THAT BUILD A BUSINESS

After the meeting

Each month, Willie meets with his members on an individual basis. This is a great opportunity to dive into the specifics of his members' companies and do what he does best and loves doing — being curious and digging.

Carrie isn't sure what to expect from her new appointment with Willie. It was a whirlwind month with the fire, meeting Willie, and spending a couple of hours with some incredible leaders. She was still digesting the range of perspectives and information. She wasn't sure she was up for another meeting with Willie, but she realized she wasn't where she wanted to be in her entrepreneurial journey. She knew to get somewhere new, she had to do something different.

Carrie walked into the coffee shop and saw Willie was just finishing up with a man who looked like he should be sitting on a beach. He was in khaki shorts, a Hawaiian shirt, and flip-flops. As Carrie approached, the man and Willie stood up to greet her. Willie introduced him as Gene, the COO of a $500 million technology company. Given Gene's attire in the middle of what she saw as a "work day," Carrie had many questions. Was Gene good at what he does? Was he just let go? Who runs a $500 million company in flip-flops? But before she could get the first one out, Willie asked, "So, what did you think of your first meeting."

Carrie took a deep breath and started with what hit her the hardest. She had been trying to do too much. She was still operating with the same mindset she had when she started the company. She didn't realize how stuck she was. She was ready to QUIT! Not quit her company, but quit the roles she had in her company. She didn't want to be the de facto answer to every problem the company has. She wanted to be like the leaders she met in the meeting. They were excited about the companies they were growing and had so much hope for what they would become. She wasn't sure she wanted to be like Gene — in flip-flops on a workday — but she liked the concept of what it represented.

Willie could see why she opted for a decaf coffee. She was wired and ready to go. Since Gene's situation was stuck in Carrie's head, it was a good time to make the underlying point of what Gene actually represented: Gene runs his company instead of the company running him. He has a team he has invested in developing. His team has a team. Willie smiled and decided to give Carrie some context before he started digging:

"There are more books on how to be a great leader than I have time to count. I have come across a lot of great leaders and not-so-great leaders over the years. I have seen organizations grow and be successful despite their owners. How were they successful, even without a great leader at the top of the organization? The company had a great leadership team. Conversely, I have known great owners whose companies were stalled until they got the right leadership team in place. If I do nothing more than help you get surrounded by the right team, I will have done my job. It's not about you; it's about the people supporting you and your vision."

Leadership teams exist in every organization in one form or another, whether you have a large established team or an informal group of "go to" people. This is how the CEO gets more done in the company by doing less.

Willie said, "Tell me about your leadership team." He was not surprised when Carrie started her response with: "I've never thought of them as being my leadership team. I see them more as people I rely heavily on, and I am not sure what I would do without them. I guess they are more of a leadership circle than a team." Carrie continued to talk about each of them. Willie was impressed that she saw the difference between a team and a circle of people around her. He wanted to make sure he understood the difference from Carrie's perspective, so he asked her to clarify.

As Carrie saw it, a leadership team would be working with each other to help win the game. In her company, she was surrounded by individuals who she saw as the leaders in her company. Unfortunately, they were a circle with her as the center and biggest dependency rather than a team.

"Karen and Dave have been with me for as long as I can remember," Carrie said. "Karen is one of the most dedicated people I have ever worked with. The best way I can describe her is what you talked about in our first discussion: She is a Swiss Army knife. She manages all administrative functions, accounting, and a lot of our human resources compliance, such as workers' compensation claims. She helps onboard new employees and makes sure our interns know what they are doing each day. I have been including her in customer meetings for years. She is great with follow-up and staying in contact. She is one of the few people I know I can rely on.

"While Karen is making sure the office is running, Dave manages all the production. He is making sure our kitchen crew knows what to do every day, the recipes are being done correctly, and everything gets shipped. It was Dave's idea to create teams in the kitchen for cross-training purposes. He picked a lead for each team and has been working with each of them. A couple of them have started asking more questions about what Dave does, so he is training them. He really enjoys the teaching aspect of it."

Willie picked up on something Carrie said as she talked about Karen and Dave. It was time to start getting curious. He noticed that when she talked about Karen, she only mentioned activities and tasks. When she talked about Dave, she focused on people. Willie asked, "Carrie, who reports to you?" Carrie started listing them off: Karen, Dave, someone doing AP & AR, a bookkeeper who closes out each month, two interns, and a few other administrative people.

Willie had to ask: "You mentioned Karen was responsible for accounting and training the interns and much of the administration. Why are they reporting to you instead of her?" Without even thinking about it, Carrie blurted out, "Because they would all quit if they reported directly to Karen."

Willie was starting to get more of the picture, but he wasn't sure if Carrie could see it yet. He painted it for her: "Let's think about the fire you had. Imagine the fire was inside your office rather than inside a dryer. Go through each person who is in the building and how they would react. You can see who is picking up the hose to put out the fire, those who are running around yelling, 'Fire,' those calling 911, and those who don't even realize there is a fire. We know your first reaction: You are the first one running toward the fire, grabbing a fire extinguisher along the way and, likely, yelling at Dave to grab the other fire extinguisher, while Karen is calling the fire department. While you and Dave are helping to put out the fire, and Karen is calling the fire department, everyone else is running in circles, or they are up on another floor doing their work as they normally would. They have no idea there is a fire. You are so busy being the one to extinguish the flames, you can't see how everyone is reacting. Everyone is waiting for you to tell them what to do, but you are too busy putting out the fire. There doesn't seem to be anyone left that you trust enough beyond Dave and Karen to do things, such as clear the building or turn off the gas. While you are fighting the fire and yelling out tasks, who is taking care of the most important thing — ensuring everyone's safety? Who is ensuring the most important things are being done, so the business and the people in it can live on?"

Carrie gave Willie's question a little more thought. It made sense to have Karen continue with her current responsibilities. She had been doing them for so many years, so why change things? She could bring in an office manager for everyone to report to instead, but that would upset Karen. One thought was to bring in a director to work alongside Karen and Dave and have that individual manage most of the people. She just couldn't think of what to call the director.

Before she got too far down this rabbit hole, Willie facetiously suggested, "How about director of fire suppression?"

Unfortunately, most of us build our leadership teams in a reactive way, to solve the problems we have today, instead of proactively, to get to where we want to go. As we are growing the company, our leadership roles end up becoming the kitchen junk drawer. It is where responsibilities that don't have a clear owner go and end up being a mix of skills and personalities. Our leadership team roles and responsibilities are created piece by piece, problem by problem, instead of looking at the entire picture and projecting what we need next and in what order.

When the business starts, nothing matters except getting more business and growing revenue to sustain the company and keep the doors open. As the company grows and the revenues are there, it becomes challenged operationally. Day-to-day operations seem to be ruled by putting out fires rather than managing the business. This is the stage where clear processes and procedures and leadership beyond the founder/CEO is needed most.

This is also the stage where the founder needs someone who can reconstruct the current systems and processes, so they can be repeatable and scalable. When the founder is the one who creates most of them, they are done in a way that makes sense to the founder. That person rarely represents the typical employee who will be hired to repeat the process. For the infrastructure to scale, it needs to be easily trainable and performable by anyone with similar skill sets.

Willie gave an example: "I was coaching a financial services firm that had three administrative employees, not including the owner. Each time the founder, Nancy, talked about replacing or adding to the team, she commented that it took a full year to train someone. A full year! That is not scalable.

"Our tendency is to hire for the problems we have today rather than what we want to accomplish tomorrow. Nancy kept looking for someone to solve the day-to-day issues that were occurring and doing the tasks exactly as she would rather than finding someone who could help her get the company where it needed to be.

"I would often ask Nancy what she wanted the company to be when it grows up. Each time, her answer was, 'I don't know, but I'll let you know when I figure it out.' She was just getting through one day at a time. This was seen in how the company operated, the roles on the organizational chart, and those she hired. She hired people to solve today's problems, not tomorrow's goals."

As much sense as it makes today to solve today's problems now, in a way, we are sabotaging the future state we want for the company. We get stuck in doing what is easy and giving direction on the fly instead of stopping to ask, "What is the right thing for the future state of the company?" Or in Carrie's case, "Do I have a team that will not only prevent a fire from starting, but that also knows what to do without me there in the event one happens?"

In order for us to know what the company needs in the future, we need to decide where we want the company to go.

CHAPTER 5

Where Are You Taking the Company?

Since Carrie had the opportunity to meet other business owners and CEOs at the meeting, hear their stories, and learn about the companies they had built (and were still growing), Willie figured she had enough insight to start applying it to her own company. He continued with one of his favorite examples about the importance of knowing where a company needs to go and sharing it with those involved:

"Think of this part of the process as an architect designing what a building will look like. Imagine not having any drawings for what the end state of the building should look like. That would entail working with a general contractor and giving them daily instruction on what they are going to build each day. They don't know what it will look like, can't buy supplies in advance, and can't make sure they have the right tradespeople showing up each day. Everyone shows up to the job site, and the architect tells them what to do that day. Without knowing the end state, they don't know which general contractor to select, and they likely don't have the right people working on it. Think of how much money they are spending on the crews every day — and they likely don't have the right tradespeople there. Everyone is standing around waiting to be told what to do."

To avoid this type of situation, give some thought and planning to what you want your company to be. This could be described in revenues, market share, the range of services to offer, and so on. Ask these questions:

- Where do we want to be in the next 5 years (or 3 or 1 — pick your timeline)?
- What does success look like now?
- How are we measuring that success?

The great part about being the owner/investor is having the opportunity to dream and think about where we want the company to end up and what kind of return we want on our investment. Do we want to exit the company? Do we want to create a legacy that is passed on to our next generation? Do we want a lifestyle business (one that makes enough money to support the lifestyle the owner wants)? Each of these will have a different definition of success and path to get there. As owners, we don't need to determine the best path to get there; we need to determine where we want to end up, have a rationale for it, and build the leadership team to make it happen.

Willie could see Carrie's excitement, as she started to think about the future state of her company. She realized she was so busy working in the business, that she hadn't thought about this since she first started making recipes in her home kitchen. She hadn't thought about anything since then other than simply growing and running the business. Willie asked what her revenue goals were for the year. She said it was impossible to predict. Since they'd invested in some new machinery, they'd need to do more than last year to cover the cost. Willie asked, "How much more?" Carrie answered,

"Anything more than last year will help me make payroll, rent, and cover the payments on the new machinery."

Willie knew Carrie was a visual thinker, so he gave her a scenario: "What would happen if you asked Karen and Dave to go for a walk?" Carrie knew they would start asking questions, such as, "Where are we walking to?" Or, "For how long?" Or, "Why now?" Willie added that if they did blindly go outside and start walking around the block, they would likely stop into the office after each lap, interrupt what Carrie was working on, and ask if they could be done walking. When we don't know the destination or the purpose of what we are doing, we have no idea in which direction to go or when we have gotten there.

This is similar to what a leadership team needs to know about where you want to take a company and the goals they need to reach in order to get there. It is harder to see, since we get caught up in the day-to-day. We often don't realize the direction and clarity doesn't exist, or we don't have the right people to ask questions, such as, "Where are we going?"

There is a flow from the CEO to the leadership team to the rest of company. At the 50,000-foot level, while the CEO is creating the vision for the destination, providing clarity so everyone can see it, and removing all obstacles, the leadership team is responsible for getting the company to the destination, while the rest of the team (employees) is running the business.

"Start with where you want to take the company," Willie said. "Think big!"

Carrie had always wanted a company of a certain size. She was at about half that now, which made the math easy: She wanted to double the size of her company.

Willie had heard this from just about every business owner he'd spoken to through the years, so he was prepared for it. "OK, that's a good start," he said. "Let's use that." A few things to think about before announcing it to the team:

- **Are your goals aligned?**

If you are looking for double-digit growth and double-digit profits, these two goals may not be aligned. Growth takes investment, which takes away from profit. If your goal is 15% net operating income, there will need to be some initial investment (and lower profits) in growing the top line, or some expense and infrastructure cuts to remove expenses, which reduces the support needed to grow revenue.

- **Are your goals measurable?**

"I want more profits" or "I want the company to grow" isn't enough. Leadership teams need a measurable goal to manage to. What is the profit number in percentage or dollars? Same question for growth: How much?

- **Are you willing to support and invest where needed?**

If you are looking to double the company in three years, this will take some changes and infrastructure investments to get there. Are you willing to accept the changes needed to get the outcomes you want? A path of high growth looks different from the perspectives of talent, culture, investment, systems, and processes than one that targets incremental growth or is on a lifestyle trajectory. If your employee base is accustomed to incremental growth, they may have no desire to be in a high-growth company. Say your sales team is made up of individuals who want to barely make their sales goals working 20-30 hours a week. You want high growth to sell the company in 3–5 years. The two are not aligned, and this will likely result in your sales team completely turning over in the near future.

Willie could see Carrie thinking this through, as he talked about what it takes to actually accomplish her goal. This was a new way of thinking for her. Why we select a goal is sometimes as important as the goal itself. The "Why" can become the vision for the company and help further guide our team.

When Willie asks owners why they chose a goal, he gets a range of responses:

- "I want to sell the company."
- "I am barely breaking even, and doubling the revenues means I don't need to make any infrastructure cuts, and I can get a good return on my investment."
- "I want to be a major player in our industry/region, and in my mind, that translates to doubling the size of the company, since the biggest player is 3 times the company's current size."

Where the number comes from can affect the strategy and roadmap the leadership team puts together. That roadmap could vary greatly for each of these. Not understanding why you chose that goal or why you want to go down that path leaves them in the dark, trying to put together a puzzle without knowing what the final picture looks like.

Coming up with a goal and accomplishing it only takes three ingredients:

1. An ability or desire to have a vision and determine how that translates to goals.
2. Trust in your leadership to share where you want the company to go and why.
3. Willingness to evolve and align to support the roadmap.

Carrie thought about the growth trajectory of her company so far. She remembered when it was $100,000 in revenue. It seemed as though it went from $100,000 to $1 million overnight, followed by $2 million. She was now far beyond that, but it made sense that the next logical step would be to double the current size of the company.

Willie thought about stopping here and leaving her to think about it between now and their next session. He decided to take it a step further.

CHAPTER 6

What Do You Need Done?

Willie continued with the next question: "What do we need to get done to get to where you want to take the company?"

There are a number of methods and tools to help determine what is needed. We don't need to create the roadmap or turn-by-turn directions at this point.

Let's use "I want to double the size of my company" as an example.

Do you know if you want to do this through acquisition and need leadership with M&A and integration experience, or are you not sure at this point? You may need to start with an expert to help you figure that out before you build or augment your leadership team, so you are getting the right expertise.

Carrie stopped Willie with an off-the-cuff remark, "I'm starting to regret even thinking about doubling the size of my company." Willie reassured her that, with the right team, she wouldn't feel so overwhelmed by what is needed to get there. The timeline for getting there will also greatly influence some of these decisions. Her role is to dream, get rid of roadblocks, and make sure the team has the resources. As long as she is comfortable with each of those, the right leadership team will do the rest.

Willie could see Carrie was having a tough time picturing this. In addition to thinking about where she wanted to take the company, he asked her to think through what her company will need to look like when it gets there. He suggested the following exercise:

Start with a clean sheet of paper, as though you are building the company, division, or department from scratch. It is often easier to build a structure from nothing, and determine what you want it to be and what type of architect and general contractor you need to make it happen, than to try to get there through a remodel. Keep in mind, though: You don't need to start fresh with your leadership team; this is an on-paper exercise.

Begin with what your organization needs today and during the next 1–2 years. List the top-level areas of the company and the objectives for each (functional or otherwise). Think of objectives in terms of what needs to be accomplished. Step back, and rearrange as needed. You may have put employee legal compliance and financial stability and health of the company together in the same box, because you currently have your finance leader overseeing HR. Consider skill sets when putting the objectives into the groups. Think about what needs to be done or accomplished — this is different from a role. Once you know what needs to be accomplished, or the objectives and outcomes, you can then group them into common skill sets and roles. Once you have your objectives grouped (put into boxes if that helps you visually), add the names of your current leadership or potential leadership. Potential leadership may have some of those skills but need a couple of years of development before they are ready to own the list/box. Again, step back.

Stay focused on the work to be done — not the role, title, job description, or person. What needs to be accomplished? Keep this high level from the perspective of the leadership team. What does the leadership team need to accomplish in order to execute on your vision and accomplish the goals (or in some cases, come up with those goals based on your vision). This is where you get to decide the destination, rather than map out exactly how to get there.

Willie knew this was not an easy concept for most. It can feel like you are trying to redesign something that is already built. He explained to Carrie: "Yes, we may need to make some changes to what you have already built or add on to it. What you currently have was built for a different purpose. That purpose no longer exists, has been accomplished, and/or will have a new purpose. You now need to remodel it for your new purpose/destination. We need to know what it needs to look like now to support your vision in order to know what adjustments to make."

Carrie started listing the tasks that need to be accomplished. She was getting into the weeds with daily tasks. It started to look like a standard job description. To think longer term, Willie wanted Carrie to think about the work to be accomplished in terms of goals or results, rather than tasks and activities.

He had recently walked through a similar exercise with one of his members who wanted some help figuring out requirements for the CFO role he was refilling. The CEO had pulled out the old job description to get Willie's help with a refresh. Willie reviewed the job description and was confused. He knew the company was looking to transition its accounting system (ERP) within the next year. It also has had a lot of turnover in the accounting department, so most employees had been there less than two years. Finally, he knew the company had filed an extension on taxes, because the team led by the controller had not yet closed out the prior year's books. None of this information was part of the job description, nor were any of the company's initiatives.

Every single bullet point on the job description was a task or responsibility that any CFO and most controllers can reasonably perform. Nowhere did the job description mention the organization's plans for the upcoming year or what this role will need to accomplish. Instead, it was focused on the static, unchanging job description of a generic CFO's day-to-day activities. It was obscuring the dynamic challenges that would face a new CFO right out of the gate.

Determining who we need in the company is forward-facing, not backward-facing. Job descriptions tend to be like the kitchen junk drawer — they accumulate all the activities, gaps, tasks, and responsibilities that currently don't have a home in an organization or that need a responsible owner.

A CFO job description with a list of requirements that includes items, such as the following, is the equivalent of saying you want to buy a car that has an engine:

- Must be able to read financial reports.
- Great leadership skills.
- Participates in company strategy.

Turn these around to more actionable results for each. Think about why you have each item on the list. For example:

- **Financial reports:** *Other than reading,* does the executive need to have experience creating the reports, establishing the KPIs, identifying the gaps and areas for improvement, analyzing for margin improvement? The more specific, the better.
- **Leadership:** Be specific. Must have managed a team of at least 5. Must have established assessment and training programs. Must have created succession planning for the organization. Why does your company need "great leadership skills," and what exactly do those look like *in your specific company*?
- **Strategy:** This is the wild card every CEO wants on their executive team. The hidden danger is getting someone who is great with strategy but not so much with execution. What part of strategic planning and implementation is most important to your company?

It does take some forethought beyond creating a title and a job description. It takes knowing where you want the company to go and what needs to be accomplished to get there.

Willie could see Carrie struggling to step back and see her company in terms of goals and objectives rather than tasks and activities. Since he didn't have a speaker for the next group session, he decided to lean into the topic he knew many of his members had struggled with. It was a good opportunity for Carrie to step away from her situation and hear about what others were going through.

Carrie had carved out some time that month to digest her conversation with Willie and the information he'd shared. She was intrigued by the finance examples. She had started to make some notes on what needed to be accomplished in the company, and the finance items had her name next to all of them. She was self-taught when it came to company finances and dreaded every moment she had to spend with Karen going through the accounting to get accurate financial statements. The more she thought about what she was good at and enjoyed doing, the more she realized finance and accounting were not on that list.

Carrie did some additional research and was surprised at how many resources were available to have someone other than herself own the goal of accurate and timely financial statements.

She started to get excited. She thought back to the past two months since the fire. Her initial goal was to figure out how to get her team to put out any future fires. She was now considering having someone else own finance and accounting. She kept reminding herself that she could still own the company while other people own the objectives and outcomes. Her dread for Willie's first meeting, which she almost tried to back out of twice, was replaced with anticipation for the next one. She wasn't quite to the point of "flip-flop Fridays," but she was on her way.

CHAPTER 7

Whom Do You Need to Do It?

A few weeks later, Willie was starting his monthly meeting with what he loved doing most. He set the stage for the discussion. He knew this would be a good discussion for a couple of members in the group who were at an inflexion point with their business, not just Carrie.

When building leadership teams, it's not about getting stars in every position. It's about getting the relevant experience for what we want to accomplish. You could bring in an all-star team from your industry or with major brands and experience on their resumés. Using this strategy, the company ends up with turnover, misalignment, and likely, some toxic behaviors within the leadership team.

Start with getting clarity on what your role is. Keep in mind, it isn't about what you think the company needs you to do. You can hire for any gaps that exist. Where can you provide the company with the highest value for your time and what you will be happy doing?

Carrie remembered this from the last meeting and the background Logan had shared. "What am I good at? What do I enjoy doing?" She smiled just thinking about it and some of the options she had started to vet for having someone else own finance and accounting. As she started to gain clarity on what she wanted to do, she was also very clear on what she didn't want to do anymore.

Willie used the example of a former member of the group. He purposefully left out the CEO's name. The CEO was looking to bring in someone to lead operations. After some heartfelt and honest discussions, he realized he didn't want to be the longer-term CEO; he wanted to step out of the role in the next two years. This changed the "whom do I need" in the COO role. He decided to find a COO who had the capability and desire to grow into the CEO role and had the skills and experience to help achieve the current CEO's vision. The current CEO became a quiet investor in the background, spending most of his time traveling. The COO, Lance, eventually became the CEO. As everyone smiled, Carrie quickly put the pieces together that Lance, sitting across from her, was the COO in the story and has since become the CEO. The more she got to know the group and how each of them came to be there, the more her mind opened to the possibilities of how she could grow her company with the right team in place.

Willie reminded them of the various skill sets they need on their leadership teams for various stages of growth. For example, when companies are starting to scale, the need for someone who can create is a priority, compared with a more mature or stable company that needs to focus on training and accountability.

This was a good time to remind the group of the speaker they'd had a few months ago who talked about some common patterns in functional roles and how to align the objective the company needs with the type of experience the leader has. The human resources example was easy to remember. He took out a piece of paper and recreated it:

Primary Human Capital Objectives	What the Objective Looks Like
Audit & Compliance	Are we legal and compliant?
Organizational Design & Development	Do we have the right people in the right seats? Are they clear on their roles and expectations?
Employee Engagement	Are we keeping the people we want?

It is easy to say all these are needed. But they aren't needed all at the same growth stage of the company, unless it is a turnaround. There also may be some specific projects or key initiatives that need to be worked on. These can include implementation of a human resources information system (HRIS) or doing a full compensation review. These are usually heavily cross-functional. This involves a very engaged leadership team in the identification and selection of who will own it. Collaboration and communication will be key. If you know there is an issue with your IT leader, and you plan to implement an HRIS system, the issue with your IT leader is not going to be resolved by bringing in the right HR leader.

Carrie stared at the list. She could see the only support she'd had in the past 10 years was in keeping the company legal and compliant. There was no one else thinking about any of the other areas, and even she wasn't giving them much thought. She wondered how many issues she was dealing with right now that could have been avoided if she had someone with experience in the other areas who could own those.

Carrie looked around and saw some of the members nodding. Bruce spoke up first and talked about the many HR leaders he had gone through before getting lucky. This was at the point in his growth when they were moving from everyone doing things differently to needing structure, systems, and processes. They needed an HR leader who could help create. The prior individuals had worked in very small companies with no structure and were great at simply keeping things going, or they had worked in larger companies where someone else put the SOP in place, and they made sure everyone was following it. At that point, he was still a couple of years (or in his case, a couple of acquisitions) away from needing a full-time HR executive working on strategy and planning. If they hired someone capable of that now, they would be overpaying for 80% of the types of activities the HR leader is working on. Instead, he worked with a very strategic HR advisor a couple of times a year, especially when doing strategic planning. The advisor also helped him better manage the HR leader they had and was a great as-needed resource.

Evette knew the value of a good HR person. She was undergoing a major transformation and needed a heavy lift on strategy, planning, and guiding their current team with implementation. There were a lot of unknowns. Fortunately, her current HR person decided she did not want to be part of the transformation and left. Rather than hiring, they used an interim HR executive who had the strategy and planning expertise and eventually helped them figure out what they need for the next stage of growth.

Willie knew the group had not always taken a straight line to figure out the leadership team they needed. He turned to Lance and asked him to share what he decided to do with human resources leadership in his company. Lance explained that no one on the leadership team wanted to lead HR. His CFO had been responsible for HR in a prior role, so he gave the responsibility to her. Willie inserted, "And how is that working out?" "Not good," Lance grumbled. "The HR manager keeps coming into my office saying the CFO is seeing the employees as numbers on paper and is questioning why we are paying people a certain way, when the only response the HR manager has is, 'Because the law says so.' The HR manager is so frustrated, she's about to quit. I recently dug into my CFO's background with HR a little bit more. My CFO had a very developed and strong HR department reporting to her as a dotted line with a solid line up to a global head of HR. I was so excited to have someone volunteer to own the problem, I didn't stop to ask the right questions."

Logan spoke up, "At least you didn't spend six figures on a vice president of IT to learn the valuable lessons of asking the right questions." For the benefit of some of the new people in the group, Willie asked Logan to provide some background on his comment. Logan had hired a vice president of IT last year. The executive's resumé was strong. It hit all the background and keywords Logan wanted. The interviews could not have gone better. Logan felt like he had just duplicated himself. They got along so well that they were practically finishing each other's sentences. The VP of IT started work, and by the third month, Logan was not happy. Within six months, Logan was past the point of trying to make it work and called it quits with the executive he was so excited about six months prior. In the end, Logan realized the individual he hired with the impressive background was previously able to accomplish it all with a large team and lots of infrastructure. Logan's company wasn't to the point of needing that type of infrastructure and scale. He needed someone who was familiar with the next growth stage of his company and could help him figure out his next evolution. The VP of IT he had hired was at least four growth stages ahead of what he needed right now. This was a difficult lesson learned, especially since Logan liked him so much.

It is easy to find people like us. These are the individuals who will think like us, say "yes" to all our great ideas, and give us more of what we already have. It was easy for Logan to see the VP of IT came from bigger companies where the strategy was done by the CIO, and the systems and standards were already set up. Logan needed someone who could tell him what he will need a year from now and to create standardization that currently didn't exist. After hearing these experiences, Carrie felt a little better that she wasn't the only one who had work to do on building her leadership team.

Willie was happy to see the group share both their successes and some of their lessons learned. It was as helpful to those who shared as it was for Carrie to hear.

Willie knew there were some additional gold nuggets the group had before wrapping it up. He went around the room and asked each person to provide their biggest piece of advice or lesson learned when identifying leadership for their company. The ones that stuck in Carrie's mind were:

- Find people who act like an owner, even when they aren't.
- Team members need to understand across the organization, not just their functional area. Everyone needs to understand the market, competitors, and customers, as well as how the company will grow (organically or by acquisition), and how they would do it as a team. You can't have people who want to stay in their lane. If you are in operations, you should still be engaged with the customers.
- Leadership team attributes: diversity, collaboration, vulnerability, values alignment.
- Collaboration, communication, alignment.
- You need honesty, and everyone needs to be able to raise their hand. This takes a lot of prompting initially, but when you get there, it is golden.

Willie wrapped up the meeting with some closing remarks:

"The importance of getting clarity of where we are taking the company, of what we need to get there, and of whom we need to have in place to accomplish it will be an ongoing exercise at each inflexion point of a company's growth.

"The more purposeful we are with this formula and process, the fewer zigs and zags we will have with our leadership team and our company. This gives us the opportunity to plan ahead to help our team grow with the company and not have the company outgrow the team. It helps guide the ongoing conversations about that growth and align the skills a company needs with the skills someone has. This is the basis for career pathing and succession planning. The foundation of these discussions is setting expectations."

Carrie digested this. What stuck in her head were the questions Willie asked her to think about before their next meeting: "Is what I need done going to get us where we need to go? Do I have the right people to get there?"

Carrie knew she had taken a big step with her willingness to bring in the finance and accounting skill sets and experience she was going to need. Beyond her desire to not do it anymore, she was going to need some additional expertise to support her growth plan that did not currently exist in the company and was far beyond anything she knew.

There were some other gaps she had been ignoring and either making up for herself or doing without. She had made some progress, but she knew there was still a lot of work to be done.

Pulling It All Together

Things to Know

- As owners, we don't need to determine the path for company growth; we need to determine where we want to end up, have a rationale for it, and build the leadership team to make it happen.
- We want to proactively build teams based on where we want the company to go, rather than to reactively solve today's problems.
- A leadership team works together to drive the company forward; a leadership circle or operating team focuses solely on getting and filling orders.
- As a company grows, systems and processes need to evolve to be repeatable and scalable, so they can be easily done by someone other than the founder, CEO, or original creator.
- When identifying what needs to be done, we should tie it to what needs to be accomplished rather than daily activities and responsibilities.
- We can own the company while other people own the objectives and outcomes.

Questions to Ask

- Am I running the company, or is the company running me?
- Do I have a leadership team or a leadership circle (a.k.a., an operating team)?

- Does my leadership team have a team, and so on?
- Where do I want to be in the next 5 years (or 3 or 1 — pick your timeline)? What does success look like? What does success look like now, and how are we measuring it?
- What do I need done to get there?
- Whom do I need to do it?
- Do I have the right people to get there?

Exercise

To determine who on your existing team can own which initiatives and where there are gaps.

- What needs to be accomplished, i.e., initiatives, objectives?
- Group the answers into common skill sets and roles.
- List current leadership in each group matching their skill sets.

Next Step: Taking Action

- Decide where you want to take the company.
- Determine what you need done to get there.
- Decide whom you need to get it done.

Section 3: GROWTH STRATEGIES: COMPANY AND EMPLOYEES

"What got you here won't get you there."

These wise words from Marshall Goldsmith rolled through Willie's head as he drove to meet with Carrie for their monthly one-to-one. Willie knew this was going to be one of the toughest conversations so far for Carrie. He knew Carrie loved the ocean, so he had her meet him at the beach for a walk. When she arrived, he did a quick check-in to see how she was doing.

Carrie updated Willie on her progress. She started by talking through some of the responsibilities she has taken on over the years and did not want to do anymore. Like Logan, she did not enjoy repetitive tasks. She did not enjoy diving into the details, and as much as she enjoyed training and developing people, she did not enjoy confrontation.

She was starting to see everything it would take to grow her business to double where it is today. She knew she could build out the physical capacity for it within their current building and some options she had for additional space. She could also see that making more product and simply doubling everything was not going to be the solution for scaling to that size. She knew she didn't have the right team in place to create the path to get there and accomplish the goals without her directing them each step of the way.

Circling back to her comment about not enjoying confrontation, Carrie wondered about how she would get from where she is today to where she needs to be, knowing she is going to have to address her fear of conflict.

Willie was ready for this discussion. Rather than jumping in and addressing her question right away, he wanted to make sure they were both on the same page.

He pointed out that when a company is starting or is in its early stages with minimal cash flow, those involved in the business are the founder(s), likely specialists in the product or service (not necessarily function), and generalists who are wearing multiple hats. This is when you want your team to be a mix of Swiss Army knives and technical experts. This is when it is very challenging to attract leaders who have experience scaling companies, since they may not be interested in being a generalist and doing a little bit of everything. But in time, the company needs those generalist roles to morph into functional specialists. He could see the question on Carrie's face, so he answered it without her having to ask. He explained that a technical expert knows your product and your industry, or they have a specific skill, such as an engineer. A functional expert has a business-oriented expertise, such as finance, marketing, or sales.

"Think back to the conversation on objectives and what needs to be accomplished," Willie said. "When the company is just starting, the same individual — a generalist — can get the marketing off the ground, work with customers to close accounts and ensure they stay customers, and manage the product specialists. As the company grows, each of these will need deeper knowledge and more specialized skills to drive, not just support, the company's next stage of growth. Sometimes the leaders in those roles morph, too, but other times, they don't."

Carrie had become very familiar with this progression. She now better understood the reason behind some of her frustrations the past couple of years. She knew the roles some members of her team were in were miles from the roles they had been hired for. She had a good idea why Willie had started the conversation this way, but she wanted to be sure, so she asked, "Where are you going with this?"

Willie continued: "As our companies grow, not everyone involved grows at the same rate or in the same direction as the company. With the planning we have discussed, we can do what we can to help them grow together. This includes setting expectations and developing them as leaders."

CHAPTER 8

Setting Expectations

Carrie had started their conversation with the self-awareness that she did not like confrontation. Willie wanted to give her a new perspective that what she saw as confrontation could be turned into a conversation around alignment. For people to grow with the company, they need to know what is expected of them.

Willie was reminded of one of the operations executives in his leadership roundtable. Giselle joined a new company last year where there wasn't much expectation management or forward-looking development.

The CEO, Joe, was still doing all the purchasing and inventory control with 30 employees. Joe hired Drew to take over purchasing, while he continued to be the point person for sourcing. As the company grew, Joe couldn't continue to be involved in sourcing, and Drew was the natural fit. Drew got more involved, and as more individuals were hired to help him, his responsibilities and title grew to vice president of supply chain. The company eventually grew to $100 million. When Giselle was brought in as the new COO, she evaluated all aspects of the operations and the leadership team. Giselle had worked with multiple manufacturing companies. These experiences included working with newly acquired manufacturing companies within a large company. Her expertise was evaluating, integrating, standardizing, and helping to create value from the investment. This was one of the things that attracted Joe to Giselle's experience. She knew what a $100 million manufacturing company should look like, as well as how to stabilize it, then set it up for the next stage of growth.

After spending time with Drew, Giselle quickly saw the value the CEO saw in him. He was a hard worker, would take on anything that was asked of him, and knew every product they bought and used on a daily basis. Unfortunately, the company had outgrown its ERP system years ago, and not much had changed about their supply chain as it grew from $10 million to $100 million. Drew and his team were now doing 15 times more work due to inefficiencies, he was taking on the extra workload from some of the underperformers, and there wasn't any potential leadership talent in his area. The company had outgrown Drew's capabilities in purchasing and inventory control a couple of years ago. At this point, his role was likely 2–3 levels above his skills and capabilities. With no expectations set, the company failed to help him grow with the company. Given Drew's current salary, it was going to be tough to transition him back to a role that aligned with his current abilities. Giselle knew there was no easy solution, but it was nothing she hadn't worked through before. She would need to understand Drew's willingness to learn and adapt. Drew had a lot to offer the company, especially as they transition to a new system.

As we promote people or hire them into leadership roles, we want to provide clear expectations and ongoing feedback on their performance against those expectations. When we first identify the outcomes we need for a role, we can make the outcomes part of the expectations. This aligns the performance expectation to our company vision, strategy, and goals with very little additional effort. It also helps streamline the performance-evaluation process. By turning the expectations into agreements with the leadership, it gives a framework for what is measured and the ongoing discussions of performance against expectations. Keeping this as a regular discussion (weekly or monthly) removes the dreaded process of annual performance reviews and the confrontational discussions Carrie avoided at all costs. Everyone knows where they are performing compared with what is expected of them on an ongoing basis.

A wise business coach once said, "Titles don't equal entitlement." A prince is entitled to the throne and, eventually, to be king. A director of operations isn't entitled to become vice president of operations. The title needs to be earned, rather than bestowed as a progression based on time with the company.

Carrie was starting to understand this perspective. Her approach and perspective were contributing to the confrontation she was wanting to avoid. This was new for her. She appreciated some detail on those forward-looking discussions. Willie explained that when expectations aren't discussed up front and on an ongoing basis, it becomes more and more difficult to discuss them. Here is an example of how to communicate it up front:

"We are bringing you in (or promoting you) to lead our operations. We expect it to grow and evolve as the company grows and evolves. We'd like to give you an opportunity to grow and evolve with it, but we can't promise what your future career path will look like. We'll keep an ongoing discussion of what is needed and expected, and where you are. We'll support you with development and training that will help you succeed either with our company or another."

Lean into a career discussion that isn't necessarily confined to your company. The employee's career path with or without the company matters as much as what the company needs.

Whether we know what we will need next at this point or we don't, we want to set an expectation of company growth, role growth, and employee growth. The importance of having clarity on this is also for the purpose of communicating it to the rest of the organization and stakeholders. The more consistent our communications and messaging are for business decisions, talent adjustments, and hires, the easier it is for our teams to connect with the path we are on, and get on board or self-select out of the journey.

For example, "We will be bringing an operations leader into the organization who is great at creating SOP, implementing, training, and accountability. We need to create a consistent structure that can scale, including operations."

Carrie could see the pieces coming together, and it made a lot of sense to her. These types of conversations were always tough for her, since she didn't have the experience leading a company through its various growth stages and never knew how to approach it. She saw how having the conversation up front and then ongoing would let her be more proactive with her company about what she expects of her team.

Carrie wanted to summarize it out loud to both validate and reinforce her understanding and perspective at this point. "If my next growth goal is to double the size of the company, I need to think through how to accomplish it and validate what is going to be needed to do it," she said. "I am going to need a leadership team that can help me figure this out and put the pieces in place to accomplish it. I understand this is going to take some time, and there are steps to get there. I have some thoughts on who is going to be able to help, who will be supportive of it, and who is going to want to fight me every step of the way. When I lead with the outcome I want and talk through what it will take, I can see how the discussion will naturally lead to their role in getting us there."

Carrie knew she had some great individuals who were likely capable but did not have the skills and experience yet to both support the growth and help drive it. She wanted to get Willie's thoughts on what to do in those instances.

Willie was impressed with Carrie's openness to see herself and her company differently. He was excited to talk about his favorite topic: developing leaders.

CHAPTER 9

Developing Leadership

In sales, the mantra is, "Always be doing business development." For strong, successful companies, the mantra is, "Always be developing leaders."

Willie was an avid proponent of making every attempt possible to develop leaders, whether you are getting them ready for what the company may need in two years, or they are already in the position.

He had a strong senior human resources leader, Don, in his executive leadership roundtable who was brought in by an investment firm to help guide a first-time CEO to grow and develop his leadership team after an acquisition. It was a privately owned manufacturing company with single-digit growth. The executive team had been there 10–20 years. That meant the least tenured member of the leadership team had been there for a decade. They were very comfortable. Along came an investment firm, bought the company, and replaced the owner with the intention of double-digit growth. The new CEO, Michael, was a first-time CEO. He was gung-ho and did not have the time or patience to let others catch up. His tendency was, if you don't get it, get off the train. But in reality, the company needed those people. There was a lot of historical/tribal knowledge. Michael brought in several new executives, including Don.

Michael's initial thought was that he needed to clear the prior team out, but Don felt they should give the legacy leadership a chance. Of the 12-person executive team, half were legacy and half were new. Yes, there was tension. Don spent a lot of time with the CEO on coaching individuals and coaching the team. They needed to move from being a holding company to being an operating company. Don got the team exposure to the financial sponsor (the investment firm). He got everyone out working with the customers. Once they got out of the offices, got exposure to the sponsor, and worked with the newer team members, they better understood what was expected and the path forward. The CFO and chief legal officer came along to what the company needed and expected of them within 18 months. It was a lot of work on their parts, but they were grateful for the opportunity and guidance to grow and develop. They were actually leading now. As a leadership team, they were able to meet the financial sponsor's goals through organic growth.

Few people have natural, instinctive skills for the roles in which they are successful. When we elevate people to roles, we want to elevate their skills, as well. They need to be educated, trained, and developed. This applies to business owners, founders, and CEOs, as well as investors.

Willie knows from experience that coaching first-time CEOs to invest in developing their leadership team often feels like he has to talk them into it. He pointed out that Don was a seasoned executive often brought in by investors who are looking to maximize their investment.

Willie suggested Carrie reach out to a couple of members of the group to hear directly from them. He had a couple in mind. Carrie quickly contacted them and was looking forward to learning more about their backgrounds and how they got to where they are.

The first was Eduardo. Eduardo had been working with Willie for a few years and wanted to support Carrie as a new member of the group.

Carrie recounted her last discussion with Willie. She updated Eduardo on her growth plans, her thoughts on what it was going to take to get there, and some gaps she had with her current team. Eduardo smiled and could see where she was in her journey.

Eduardo started his business 13 years ago. Before that, he worked in a corporate role where he had staff under him, and he could work at a higher level and focus on what he is good and competent at. When he first started his business, he didn't have the budget he'd had in his corporate role. He hired people who had value alignment but very little competence (experience and skills). He figured, if he could get value alignment, he could train them on the rest. Then he had breaking points. His company was growing, and he was trying to grow an executive team from those he had. Unfortunately, everyone has a level of elasticity, and it can end up snapping. He put people in positions where they'd fail. He would have big spurts of growth that outgrew their competencies. It was frustrating for everyone involved.

In the beginning, he had a lot of fear of investing in the right people and then having them leave. He recognized he needed redundancies — including duplicating himself. He stopped growing from within and started hiring executive-team members from outside companies that were 3 times his size, and he understood what systems, people, processes, and technology needed to be in place to support the growth. He made sure to assess their ability to create and implement the systems. When hiring for experience at companies larger than his, he understood the difference between leaders who could operate in a systematic environment vs. leaders who could put the systems in place. He hired for the second.

He hired two strong leaders, including someone to lead operations, which is not his strength. He liked the idea of having an integrator in the company to complement his visionary tendencies. Both leaders have a lot of experience in his industry and came from competitors, but even so, he realized everyone needs development, including himself. He needed to adjust from telling them what to do to providing the resources for what they know they need to do. His role is to give guidance and manage the vision, so they can surpass what he knows and share it with others. He is learning to support them and not be as reactive or stepping in to tell them what to do.

Eduardo has learned that, beyond value alignment, the company needs competence. They also need career paths and continual learning. His brother was in the military for 30 years, and he realized the military does something similar. At the leadership level, a common practice is to send individuals for training or to school for two leadership roles ahead of where they are. They take what they learned into their next role, go to school again, and by the time they take on each role, they have had years of development, training, and exposure to various roles. This is not feasible or applicable to most organizations, but there are pieces of it that can be applied.

It is a constant learning curve, and Eduardo has made all the mistakes. He is a different leader than he was when he started. It is a conscious decision to join various peer groups with outside perspectives, so he can grow the company and not have it outgrow him. He thought about bringing in someone else to run the company for him, but he decided that, as long as he was having fun building the team and developing leaders and himself, he enjoyed being the one to run it.

Carrie hadn't given much thought to the fact that, as an owner/CEO, she was in a role she had never been in before. She was so caught up in the day-to-day of "figuring it out." She could relate to Eduardo's point about making mistakes and learning from them. She asked Eduardo more about where he learned all this. He chuckled, thinking about the years of learning that has contributed to his knowledge base. He had seen many scenarios during his time in corporate jobs, and he learned from listening to other members of peer groups, books he has read, and speakers. Carrie wasn't looking for her learning curve to take years. She needed to speed it up a bit.

She decided to pick his brain on a couple of scenarios that greatly resembled her own situation and team. "I have a really strong food scientist named James," she said. "He has expressed interest in wanting to grow within the company, but I am having a tough time seeing him as something other than a food scientist. I just don't know if it is the right thing for him or the company."

Eduardo remembered this type of situation from his private-equity days, when he'd evaluate leadership teams. It was common for individuals who have a very specific skills set, such as engineers. He referred to them as a subject matter experts (SME). They have a strong command of their area of expertise. As leaders, we need individuals who understand the impact of decisions across the organization, can read a P&L, manage a budget, develop people, and create a roadmap for future growth. As you develop an SME to understand and gain these competencies and general leadership skills, they will become less of an SME. Keep the discussions very open and sincere as to how they feel about this. As owners, we have a tendency to promote SMEs quickly, because they are such great employees. They may not want to lose their SME status and enjoy being that expert in the company. It also comes naturally for them, making it more difficult to teach others they are leading. Do they have a curiosity for how other parts of the company operate and work together? Do they enjoy new challenges and working with others as a team, compared with being an individual contributor?

If they have the desire to learn and grow and align well with your culture, developing someone like that into a future leader of your company is one of the most rewarding things you can do as an owner.

Carrie could see the development path for James, and she was excited to start some informal discussions with him. Carrie really enjoyed working with clients. She loved going to trade shows, meeting new people, getting introduced to new recipes, and figuring out how to make them come to life in a new brand on the supermarket shelf or favorite item on a restaurant menu. The parts she enjoyed were identifying the opportunities to help and getting the relationship started. She knew she would need more people-oriented individuals to support clients throughout the relationship. Fortunately, these types of individuals were plentiful in her industry. The part of her current job that was the most difficult to replicate was the part of the job that was part science, part business. She either needed to compete inside the industry for those who could do both or develop someone, such as James, who can lead specialists in each area and bring the two together. He was a great scientist and seemed to have a good head for business. She was looking forward to getting other input on how she can support his growth.

Next, she shared the issue that had been nagging her for some time: "Since Willie and I first started talking, he has mentioned a generalist or Swiss Army knife a couple of times. I have someone who has been with me almost since the beginning, and she can do just about anything I throw at her. She is also one of my highest-paid team members. I'm not sure what to do with her or her role at this point. I am really struggling with how to align her value to the future growth of the company with her abilities."

Eduardo knew that situation all too well. "This is the opposite of what we just discussed," he said. "In this situation, you are developing a generalist into a functional leader. They helped hire people, onboarded, showed them how to use the coffee machine, made sure vendors got paid, unloaded trucks in the warehouse when needed, and planned the annual company picnic. One of the first questions to ask is whether they want to be a leader. Being willing to take on anything you ask them to do is different from wanting to help lead the direction of the company and develop career paths for those in it. Remember the discussion from our last meeting? Think through that list from strategy to accountability to tasks. Have a lot of open discussion and evaluation on where her strengths are and are not.

"Once you decide where you want your company to go and the skills needed to get there, you can talk through the expectations of current and future roles with her. If this isn't your strength, work with a consultant or outside expert to identify the gaps between what the company needs and the individual's existing skills and experience. Identify training courses and peer groups they can attend. If everyone is aligned on the potential of the individual, you can also bring someone in from outside the company to the leadership team on a temporary or part-time basis. One of the expectations may be to mentor the future leader. They aren't going to be that leader tomorrow, and that should be part of your expectation-setting discussion, as you discuss the development plan."

There was something nagging Carrie. "Eduardo, you mentioned you have a director of operations you are looking to develop into your COO, as the company grows and needs it," she said. "You said you came from finance, not operations. Since you haven't been a COO of a company, how much do you know about developing someone to be a COO."

Eduardo grinned and answered honestly: "Very little. I know what the COO I will need looks like, and I know how to develop someone into a leader. I likely am going to have her work with a coach who has been a COO and can support her behind the scenes. She is a hands-on learner, so I think someone with whom she can talk through situations, prep for meetings and discussions, and get real situational feedback will help her the most in her growth. Granted, these are just my thoughts. She and I have started to have these discussions, and I've asked her to think about it."

Carrie thought Eduardo had made a good point. In each of these scenarios, it is important to ask what individuals on the team want and discuss how she can help them get there. She wanted to be careful not to get so focused on what she wanted for people that she forgets to check in and take their temperature on their desire for development within the company. Carrie made a mental note to get James' thoughts on his desire to go from being an individual contributor to managing others.

Eduardo continued: "When identifying future leaders in our company and developing them over time, this is the least costly and straightest line to building a leadership team that can build your company. There may be some hidden gems inside the company. They understand your customer base, are already nurturing others, and are helping the company succeed. As we discuss getting alignment with the current leadership team or identifying misaligned individuals, keep your eyes and ears open for those voices in the company that may have been previously silent. This is one of the first places turnaround CEOs go for ideas on growth opportunities or operational efficiencies. They already have the knowledge; they just need the opportunity to grow. Sometimes you need to change the rules to give them a chance."

Carrie let Eduardo know how much she appreciated his time and went back to the office to focus on what still needed to get done that day. More and more, she was looking forward to "flip-flop Fridays" any day of the week.

CHAPTER 10

When One Outgrows the Other

Carrie had breakfast scheduled a few days later with another member of the group, Greg. She had been mulling over her conversations with Eduardo and Willie. The more she talked through her growth goals, what it will take to reach them, and the skills and experience she needs to accomplish them, the more one individual on her team stood out in her mind.

She gave Greg an overview of her prior conversations and talked about what had been top of mind for her.

Greg shared his background with a similar situation. But in his situation, the individual was the business partner he started the company with and was as close as a family member.

They had been partners for 20 years and had many amazing life experiences together. Even outside the business, if they made an investment, it was together. It was a tight relationship. When they first immigrated to the U.S., they were sharing an apartment with a handful of other guys, learning the language, and struggling to build a business when they didn't have business experience.

They reached a point when it was clear to Greg that his partner was good at building the company — he'd run to Home Depot when something needed to be fixed, look for an office, buy equipment. Once they went beyond $1 million to $10 million, it became frustrating. As owners of the company, they needed to be focusing on how to grow and create a scalable infrastructure. The partner wanted to continue to do the activities that were within his skill sets, which included running errands and doing administrative tasks. It made it hard for the organization to take the next step.

How do you grow a company while keeping everyone happy? At some point, you cannot do both 100%. Greg had moments where he felt there was no solution. He believed loyalty came first.

He learned, though, that it isn't about it being anyone's fault; it's about the company getting to the next level. Once Greg got that clarity, it opened the gate for looking forward. Eventually, he had an honest, open conversation with his business partner.

It helped to make the conversation objective and centered around the company instead of the individual. For example, say the company is making $10 million in revenue, and they want to go to $20 million in the next two years. The company needs better managers, structure, and processes. Is the team we have today the right team to grow the company to its next level? Ask the person where they think they have the most value to take the company through the next $10 million. When you have this objective conversation, people will start culling themselves out. They will end up at another company going from $0–$10 million again, because this is where they are best aligned. The value some people offer the business when it is smaller and the value as it grows are different. The conversation should be centered around what the company needs.

Business owners have a lot to consider. The question to ask is, "Will this person help you get to the next stage of growth?" This is a different question from, "Can this person keep up with the next stage of growth?" The leadership team needs to be the group guiding (a.k.a., leading) the way, rather than being pushed or pulled. If the answer is "no," it doesn't mean they aren't a good person or are deficient as a member of the team. It means they are missing the skills needed for the next steps. The more we plan and are purposeful about it, the more options we have for anyone who isn't ready. In the event they aren't the right fit for the next stage, it doesn't mean they aren't the right fit (and happier) somewhere else inside or outside the company.

When determining the value someone has to the leadership team, it needs to be done based on a future state, rather than the past or with legacy reasoning. Start with two separate lists. First, list what each individual on the leadership team, or those you consider to be your core team, have contributed to the growth of the business. On the second list, note what is going to be needed moving forward. Then connect the two lists.

This will help you decipher the capabilities that were important to getting the company to where it is vs. what will be needed moving forward. This may also help identify those individuals who have not been given the clarity or opportunity to contribute. They may not have had the chance to demonstrate what they are capable of. Give them a goal (preferably numeric), and give them three months. Do weekly check-ins initially. You can start to spread the check-ins out as time goes on. If there isn't alignment between their skills and the skills needed, it will become clear to both of you.

It's never going to be easy. That is why so many leaders hesitate to make tough decisions. There are countless reasons we hesitate to make personnel changes, including:

- They have a key client relationship.
- If they leave, three other people will leave.
- "They are the glue keeping things running around here."

When these run through your mind as reasons to not make the tough decision for the company, they end up emphasizing that it is the right decision. Greg remembered the salesperson who was responsible for their biggest client. There were a number of challenges and conflicts with the salesperson, even to the point of complaints from other team members. Greg did not want to imagine what would happen with their biggest client without this individual. In the end, the salesperson left for what he saw as a better opportunity. As Greg initially stepped in and met with this individual's clients, a lot of information came out that was reflective of the internal complaints. It reminded Greg of the saying, "Where there's smoke, there's fire." He quickly remembered Carrie's reasons for originally joining the group and added, "No pun intended."

When evaluating the existing and potential leadership the company needs, use the following perspectives:

- What skills do they have and how are they performing to expectations?
- What is their ability to learn and evolve?
- What is their willingness to learn and evolve?

There are tools that can help evaluate each. As an owner, you likely know 80% of it yourself. This will give you a good starting point to determine next steps with each person.

Carrie started going through the team in her head. Her gut had been telling her a lot of this; she just didn't know how to make sense of it, verbalize it, or what to do next. She knew where some of the gaps were with her team, and she had been working around them or compensating for them herself.

Greg could see the impact of the discussion setting in. Carrie wanted to know what to do next. Once any gaps are identified, there are options to help align the value members of the team can bring with what the company needs.

- **Coach**

When someone has the ability and willingness to learn, but there are some gaps in their skills that are affecting performance, coaching is a good option. There are coaching options, including peer groups, leadership development, or on-the-job training with an experienced leader, whether they exist in the organization or are brought in temporarily. This option is best for future-planning purposes and being proactive. The success ratio goes down when it is done as a reactive measure, such as after they have been put on a performance improvement plan.

- **Move**

When someone is aligned with the company culture, but either doesn't have the capabilities or willingness to gain the skills needed, moving them into another role within the leadership team or elsewhere in the organization can be an alternative. Similar to coaching, this is more viable the sooner it is recognized. Once someone is in a role a couple of steps beyond their skills and abilities, moving them to a role that is more suitable is asking a lot of both the individual and those working with the individual. It also becomes more challenging to align pay with the role and contribution level to the company. This option can have some success when someone has been elevated to a manager or leadership role and is not enjoying the responsibility of leading and developing others. They miss being an individual contributor as an SME or in a role where they are only responsible for their own output.

- **Exit**

When the company and the individual cannot get alignment on skills, ability to grow, and willingness to grow, it is time to help them move on to a situation where there is alignment. It is human nature to want alignment in life. Even when there isn't alignment within our company, we can help those individuals find alignment elsewhere. This can be at a vendor, a customer, or with someone we know. It may be a great testimonial of where their strengths and expertise are. There's additional assistance that can be offered in the form of transition coaching, as well, to help them figure out what may be a good next step or fit for them.

There are also those situations where skills don't matter, since the person isn't willing to align with the direction of the company, and/or the culture is not a fit. These are the individuals who have more "buts" in conversations than "ands." They want to be the ones controlling the storyline and messaging, creating a sub-culture within the company. They are always the victim. They are stuck in a spot where they need to have control of the situation and what is going on in the company, despite not being an owner or CEO. Since this is their way of being, it is not as coachable in a business setting. Even if they have all the key client relationships, they need to find a place where they can have control. If they are exhibiting these tendencies internally with the company, it is happening externally with the clients, as well.

As Greg shared the last example, Carrie had an unsettled feeling in her stomach. She had someone in the company who was exactly what he was describing. It became all too clear as Greg painted the picture, and she could start to pinpoint the impact it was having on the rest of the team. Dave had brought it up a few times, but Carrie wasn't ready to see it herself. In these situations, once you see it, you can't unsee it. Carrie took a deep breath and exhaled loudly.

Greg saw Carrie's shoulders relax a little, as though a weight had started to come off. He asked who else in the group she was planning to meet with. He was surprised that she was packing in three meetings in such a short period of time. Carrie explained she was feeling like she was in the middle of a rope bridge with a deep ravine below. She wanted to get across that bridge as quickly as possible and was looking for as much information and insights as she could get. She was having lunch with Jeanette tomorrow.

Jeanette was fascinating. Carrie was hanging on every word about the various companies she had worked in and leadership teams she had been part of. In contrast to Eduardo and Greg, Jeanette was not an owner of her current company. At her past two companies, she'd joined as a member of the leadership team and ended up as president of the first and, now, CEO of the second.

At the first company, Jeanette came in as the chief revenue officer. The owner/CEO had built the company for 20 years into an amazing company but recognized he needed something different to continue to grow it. After a year with the company, the CEO asked Jeanette to step in as president. She quickly figured out one of the biggest constraints was the VP of sales, who had been there 17 years. He was not working for what the company needed at this stage of growth. The CEO knew it but feared what would happen if they made any changes. Jeanette assured him it would be fine. Once he trusted her to make that decision, it was a turning point. There was some fallout, but when stories started coming out about issues that had been created by him, they knew the right decision for the company had been made.

It was easier for the super-passionate founder/CEO to drive change through Jeanette. They would discuss, she would agree or challenge him, and they would come to the right thing for the company. She would then drive the change. She was able to alter the founder's relationship with work.

She brought in an HR professional. HR had been a support center, and she wanted it to be a business driver. It was more than the CEO previously had spent on HR, but within one month, he saw the value. Jeanette also became the buffer between the founder and the rest of the team. She was the numbers person, and the HR professional was the people person, so they made a good team.

With her current company, Jeanette has not changed one leader. Instead, she has adjusted their roles, and they are still with the company. The CEO when she joined was one of the founders and part owner; the board makes up the rest of the ownership. It was an inexperienced board that removed the CEO in a less-than-desirable way. Before coming in, Jeanette spoke to that CEO and decided she would come in as COO instead of CEO. They developed a good working relationship and were able to make the transition as smooth as possible. She eventually moved into the CEO role, and he is now consulting, doing what he does best. He built the company. He is an entrepreneur and really wanted to go build another company.

When Jeanette started, there were people with titles. Though there was a formal leadership team, there wasn't a group working together, making decisions, debating, setting strategy, and solving problems. One of the first moves she made was to shift the VP of production to VP of facilities. He was initially hired for compliance and then promoted to VP of facilities. In his role as VP of production, he is the best she has now.

She moved the VP of client services to VP of operations. He was amazing in that role, and now he is the COO. It was a great fit.

As an owner, Carrie was curious about how the existing team felt about Jeanette coming in from the outside. They had helped build the company to that point, and now someone was going to come in and tell them what to do. Jeanette understood that perspective all too well. It was a valid concern. Jeanette has seen it done well and not done well. She has learned to respect what the company and the people in it have done up to that point. The term "legacy" comes up a lot when talking about the past and what got the company to that point. At the same time, the company, and the people leading it, need to evolve so the company can grow.

Of course, this doesn't mean you should dismiss everything that got the company here and start doing everything differently. The past should be respected but placed in proper context. A lot of acquisitions fail here. Change needs to happen, and successful CEOs are able to determine what part of the legacy should be kept, what can be evolved, and what needs to be replaced.

From Jeanette's experience, the most important element is communicating the direction in which the company is going and why. This is where alignment and integrity continue to play leading roles. Once the direction of the company is set, the decisions must be consistent with this direction, from what products or services the company invests in, to onboarding and off-boarding decisions.

It is not uncommon for the vision and direction of a company to change, which also changes the circumstances for most involved. When the vision, strategies, and goals of the company are clearly communicated, and the decisions and actions that follow are aligned with this, it minimizes surprises. The path should be so clear that the team knows what is coming next. The more we communicate where the company is going and what is needed to get there, the more the team has the opportunity to decide whether they want to be on board.

When decisions and changes being made are in alignment with where the company is going, it builds trust and understanding with the team. It gives the leadership team the opportunity to determine how to get there, make plans, determine gaps and needs within their teams, and celebrate the milestones on the way to accomplishing the goals. When these are not clear or are changed often without the consultation of the leadership team, it breeds mistrust and misalignment.

Carrie still had a gnawing feeling, so she asked, "What if there is someone who doesn't fit, but you just can't imagine moving the company forward without them?"

Jeanette could see the concern in Carrie's face. Jeanette answered: "Ah yes, the sacred cow. Sometimes there is an individual who has reached the peak of their skills and abilities with the company, and you have decided to keep them anyway. Their contribution to the company is not aligned with their compensation, and you have decided not to change this. This is then a conscious decision to make room in the budget for the individual. There does need to be some communication on the individual's role to limit the impact of this decision on other areas of the organization."

Jeanette thought for a few moments and decided to add one more piece of advice: "One thing to remember: People in the organization pay very close attention to behaviors. It's not what you say, but what you do. People think CEOs always have the answer. First-time CEOs often want to have all the answers. If you do, then you aren't relying on your team for their expertise. It is OK to admit you don't have all the answers.

"As leaders, we want to build a foundation of trust and alignment with our leadership team. What can sometimes come across as the company outgrowing individuals on the leadership team can actually be symptoms of misalignment within the leadership team. While you are evaluating who you want and need on your leadership team, be conscious of possible misalignment with existing team members."

Carrie made a note to discuss team alignment further with Willie at their next meeting, and she thanked Jeanette for all she had shared. Her gnawing feeling had gone from internal conflict to resolution regarding the discussion she needed to have with Karen. She knew the company had evolved and grown since Karen was hired. Karen really enjoyed doing a little bit of everything and figuring it out as she went. Carrie could see how helpful that was in the beginning stages of the company's growth, but she now understood it could end up hurting the company and frustrating Karen going forward. She was curious how Karen would feel about Carrie's growth plans for the company — once she gets over the initial shock that there's actually a plan.

Carrie realized she was growing and evolving, as well, and was enjoying the journey. She had a much better idea of how to structure the discussion, giving Karen some background on where she wanted to take the company, why, and some of the milestones they would need to reach. Carrie planned to share more about what she enjoys doing and those activities she doesn't plan to do anymore. It's a good opportunity to talk through the decision Carrie has made to bring in a part-time CFO to manage the finance and accounting. Eventually, she will need someone who can manage the business on a day-to-day basis. She thought of Karen like family and sincerely wanted to find a place for her that aligned with her skills and what she enjoys while supporting the company's growth.

Pulling It All Together

Things to Know

- Setting expectations: Everyone knows how they are performing compared with what is expected of them on an ongoing basis.
- Align performance with company vision, strategy, and goals.
- Always be developing leadership.
- When evaluating the existing and potential leadership the company needs, use the following perspectives:
  - Skills and performance
  - Ability to learn/evolve
  - Willingness to learn/evolve
- Options for existing leadership: Coach, Move, Exit

Questions to Ask

- Do I have a leadership team that can drive the company forward rather than be pulled/pushed?
- Who can help get the company to the next stage of growth?
- Am I investing in developing the people who have the ability and willingness to learn and evolve?
- When evaluating potential leaders, do they have a curiosity for how other parts of the company operate and work together? Do they enjoy new challenges and working with others as a team, compared with being an individual contributor?

Exercise

To decipher the capabilities that were important to getting the company to where it is vs. what will be needed moving forward.

- Start with two separate lists.
- First, list everyone on the leadership team, or those you consider to be your core team, and what they have contributed to the growth of the business.
- On the second list, note what is going to be needed moving forward. Then connect the two lists.

Next Steps: Taking Action

- Communicate the direction the company is going in and why. Keep decisions consistent with this direction, from what products or services the company invests in, to onboarding and off-boarding decisions. The path should be so clear that the team knows what is coming next.
- Set clear expectations for each person on your leadership team, including objectives and how they are measured. Have ongoing discussions on progress.
- Evaluate and invest in developing your current and future leadership.

Section 4: LEADERSHIP TEAM ALIGNMENT

A few weeks later, Carrie walked into the large conference room. She thought about the difference from the first time she walked into the meeting. Beyond knowing everyone's name, she could connect with their updates, their struggles, and their successes. She was part of a community that was different from the community she'd built in her own company. She had felt so alone there, even though it was her company. She now had others she could talk to about anything that was on her mind. It was a nice feeling.

This was Carrie's third meeting. It would be the first time she'd get to listen to a speaker. She had gained so much from other members and Willie. The thought of how she would have felt a few months ago about sitting through a couple of hours of someone teaching her how to be a better leader when she could be at the office getting things done made her laugh.

The speaker's topic was leadership team alignment. Carrie wasn't sure about this. She didn't see herself as having enough of a team to have to worry about alignment at this point, but she was open to learning.

CHAPTER 11

Getting Aligned

The speaker, Steve, started the presentation with the results of a survey that asked employees about what issues they see most in their organization. Carrie noticed that the top five were centered around the direction the company is going and the leadership team. They were:

1. Detachment from the "Why"
2. Succession planning confusion
3. Recruiting and vacancy challenges (No. 1 red flag that something is wrong = turnover)
4. Outdated organization structure
5. Tensions between leaders

Steve had the CEO group focus on the last point a little more, saying it can cause a ripple effect on the others. "We can have an all-star leadership team," he said. "However, if they aren't able to work together to further the growth of the company, the rest of the employees not only see it, they also experience the fallout from it."

A misaligned team is easy to spot. There are tensions among the team, there is more gossip and personal agendas than problem solving, timelines and goals slip, blame and finger pointing are prevalent, and employee complaints and turnover are on the rise.

While not having the right leadership team can hold a company back from forward movement, a misaligned team can cause the company to take steps backward and cause real damage to the organization.

Carrie was hooked. For the next couple of hours, she filled her notebook with ideas and comments.

CHAPTER 12

Clarity

When the path isn't clear, we make our own path. In a company with a five-person leadership team, this becomes five different paths. The team needs clarity on where they need to go and each person's role in getting there. As CEOs, we give them the destination and determine who owns what part of the journey. It is their responsibility to then create the path.

Working together as a team is one of the most critical concepts in leadership. We set the example for how the rest of the company should work together toward their common goals.

Carrie felt she could write her own book based on what she has learned about clarity. She thought back to the architect example Willie had given her. She needs to make sure everyone is clear on what is being built and their role in building it.

CHAPTER 13

Consistency

Steve said there is a running joke that leadership teams dread the day after monthly meetings like this. Why? "We spend the day listening to a great speaker on a topic that provides useful information about an area of our company; we are given tools and advice," he said. "I promise today will be no different! We are excited to go back the next day and start putting these into practice. We walk in and start sharing what happened and what the speaker said. We want ideas on how to start implementing the new concepts. As much fun as it is for us to share, our teams do not share our same excitement.

"Let me give you their perspective. I had a boss like this once. I referred to his tendency to take us off track from what we were focused on as 'the good idea fairy.' The good idea fairy would visit Friday afternoons, and he wanted an update on the implementation of his new good idea first thing Monday morning."

As business owners, we tend to be visionaries. Possibilities exist in our head 24/7. We love brainstorming and talking out loud, sometimes unaware of the impact of those musings on our team — especially our leadership team.

Self-awareness is part of our development as owners and leaders. Being aware of what we do that inspires our team is helpful — as is being aware of what derails our team. When our team has a plan and can work the plan without any distractions other than those inherent in the business, we are giving them the opportunity to succeed. We are empowering our team to raise their hand when they are stuck and could use some brainstorming.

A wise turnaround executive once said, "A CEO should work on the people, not the project." Focus on the people and where they need development or roadblocks removed to achieve the goals. They, in turn, can focus on the project (a.k.a., goals).

If you are someone who loves talking out loud, brainstorming, bouncing business ideas off others, then being in a group with other leaders is a good place to work through those initial ideas. Getting input on new concepts and working through how they align with your goals with other leaders first can keep you from derailing your teams. Make sure you have clarity on those ideas, and that they are consistent with the direction of the company and what the team is currently working on before you start communicating about them.

CHAPTER 14

Communication

We communicate every day of our lives. This can be one of the most natural things next to breathing and eating. Yet, communicating effectively across our organizations is one of the areas usually in need of the most improvement.

There are a couple of parts to effectively communicating as a leadership team:

1. Communicating with each other.
2. Communicating with the rest of the organization.

As a leadership team, having a common language and guidelines for communication, especially when challenging ideas and plans, can be important. This does involve fundamental trust. If any members of the team don't feel safe, or there is an absence of trust, communication can quickly turn into unhealthy conflict.

When we are in a meeting and someone starts pointing the finger and blaming someone for a large customer order that was shorted a few key products, it is easy for others in the meeting to shut down, because they no longer feel safe or think an argument is about to start. However, if the individual responsible for the meeting simply states, "Let's be hard on the process, not the people," it can quickly reset the finger pointing and focus the discussion where it belongs: Where did our process breakdown?

Communicating with the rest of the organization involves messaging about where the company is going; how it will get there; and everyone's goals, roles, and responsibilities.

Creating a communication plan is not something leaders want to think about, enjoy figuring out, or want to spend their time doing. It generally isn't a skill set shared across a leadership team. This ends up being even more of a challenge in organizations where the HR department is compliance-oriented rather than oriented toward employee engagement and organizational development.

Though everyone on the leadership team has a responsibility to communicate, having someone own the accountability of what will be communicated, how, when, and by whom can be a game-changer. Having a two-way communication plan between leadership and the rest of the organization translates to everyone having the same map.

To make the point, Steve walked up to Carrie and whispered something in her ear. He then continued to explain what he wanted Carrie to do. The rules of the exercise sounded a bit like the telephone game from when she was a child. She wasn't sure how a game from when she was 8 was applicable to a group of leaders, but she was willing to participate. Steve reminded them the statement could only be said once, with no repeats or questions. Carrie was now kicking herself for not paying better attention when Steve first whispered the statement in her ear. She leaned over to Jeanette and continued the exercise.

It didn't take long for them to go around the table of 12 participants. Lance was last, and Steve asked him what he heard. Lance announced that a dog went to a concert, got arrested, and was in jail. Carrie was reminded why she played this game as a child. Hearing that come out of Lance's mouth with such conviction, as though he had been there partying with the dog, was the funniest thing she had heard all week. Steve asked Carrie what she heard. Carrie said something about a faucet and going to Home Depot. Jeanette turned and laughed, telling her that was absolutely not what she had heard.

Steve asked the group to speculate on how the statement, "The cat went to the store and bought a toilet," turned into a dog going to a concert and getting arrested. "You were sitting right next to each other, and there's only a dozen of you," he said. Hands shot up and the answers to what had gone awry came easily:

- There is no basis or context for what is being shared. The initial statement about a cat going to a store and buying a toilet makes no sense.
- The communication is one way. There is no opportunity to ask and get clarity about what is said. There is no opportunity to gain understanding about why in the world a cat is going to the store and why a toilet rather than a litter box.

- There is no feedback loop. There was no chance to stop the game at any time and ask what CEO No. 3 had heard, get it corrected, and go on.

Steve said: "The human brain wants to make sense of information. When it doesn't make sense, we fill in the blanks from our own experiences. When information is not provided or is not clear, we will make up our own to make sense of a situation or what we are being told.

"As we are communicating within our leadership team, take the time to talk through the communication plan and how we will create a feedback loop. This will alleviate fears and reduce individual storylines that occur in the absence of clear communication."

Steve gave some examples of communication methods:

- Leverage the statements you have put thought and effort into already: vision statement, mission statement, core values, etc. These are all powerful tools to communicate through. Since you have alignment with those statements already, tie initiatives and stories back to these.
- Give the leadership team a common presentation or talking points to walk through with their teams.
- Create two-way communication by inviting others to be part of meetings with the leadership team. They could be presenting, giving feedback, or observing to learn how to communicate effectively within their own meetings.

CHAPTER 15

Collaboration

Everyone has their own leadership style. Some involve problem solving with others, while some internalize the problem-solving process before discussing openly. Understanding how our team solves problems and works together is important to help them be aligned.

Some of the most engaged teams are those with a mission-critical initiative and timeline. Steve shared an experience of needing to hire 400 people in five different states within 12 weeks and having them trained and ready to start. What would normally have taken a minimum of 6 months was accomplished in half the time through incredible collaboration within a new leadership team. As a team, they were dependent on each other for success.

As leaders, we don't want to wait until we have a mission-critical initiative, but we can take any problem occurring in the organization and make it into a mission-critical case study. Most business situations and problem solving are done over weeks or months. It is tough to identify gaps or opportunities when the situation is spread over time. However, if it is condensed to a few hours, and you can watch it in real time, those gaps and opportunities for improved collaboration become more apparent.

If a CEO has all the answers, then they aren't relying on their team for their expertise. They aren't modeling collaboration. By showing it is OK to not have the answers and being open about it, you are setting the example for the kind of teamwork and collaboration that can mean the difference between missing goals and surpassing goals.

Steve shared two good ways to illustrate this. First, at an offsite, give the team a mission-critical initiative to solve together — and two hours to accomplish it.

A second exercise is job rotation, which is walking a day in someone else's shoes. Aligned and effective leadership teams understand what each other does, have a working knowledge of the entire organization, and take these into account within their accountabilities and responsibilities. Even though the CFO or VP of human resources is not personally accountable for sales, they should understand the industry, the markets, the customer base, and the impact of the products/services the company sells.

"I had a client that rotated the leadership team every three years," Steve said. "The CIO had no formal education or hands-on experience in information technology. However, there was a very strong technical management team that supported the CIO. The CIO had been the head of store operations prior to the role as CIO. The VP of customer service had been rotated into store operations. They each understood each other's roles from hands-on experience and knew how they needed to work together."

CHAPTER 16

Conflict

Conflict tends to have a negative connotation. As counter-intuitive as it may be, conflict is a good thing for effective and aligned leadership teams.

It can be easy to mistake disagreement for misalignment. Alignment doesn't mean we agree on all things all the time. It means we are aligned on where the company is going and how we will get there. We are aligned with our communications and how we collaborate. We share common values and are aligned on the company's culture. Defining all these and getting alignment involves challenging the way we think and how we do business. This can be done in a respectful and productive way.

Great leaders get that way by being surrounded by people with various strengths who can challenge thought processes, strategies, and plans. This should be done throughout leadership teams. To accomplish this, healthy conflict is needed. Everyone needs to feel safe to raise their hand. If this is not currently the norm, it may take some prompting.

Healthy conflict is how we innovate and move the needle of profitability. It is how we get unstuck, and how we attract and retain great talent.

CHAPTER 17

Culture

Steve saved culture for last, since it is a culmination of everything the group had discussed that day. Volumes have been written on it, and an entire industry exists to help organizations create a culture that drives the vision and mission. "Culture eats strategy for breakfast": The saying is true!

"I have seen culture driven by the CEO, and I have seen it driven by the leadership team in spite of the CEO," Steve said. "In the absence of a culture people want to join and be a part of, they will either create their own or leave. When interviewing, candidates almost always say, 'Tell me about your culture' early in the process. This becomes part of decision making for executives when deciding whether to join a company. When they are being asked to step into an organization to help solve one or more challenges, the culture tells them how heavy a lift the challenge will be."

No one was surprised when Trevor spoke up. Trevor has a sales-based organization. No one in his company makes a product; they sell a product made by other companies they source from, and they sell millions of dollars worth of it. He decided long ago that culture will be the guiding light for everything they do. This includes their market strategy, hiring, compensation, and management. As the organization has grown, it has been centered around the culture he has created. In retrospect, he knows any leadership mistakes he has made were because they weren't aligned with the culture. As he says, "We are 100% culture driven." This is how he wants to run his company and how he attracts crazy-driven salespeople who wouldn't fit into most organizations but thrive in his.

Never underestimate the value of culture when building a company, a leadership team, or anything else you want to accomplish.

Steve's presentation was on point for Carrie. As much as she didn't think it was applicable to her situation at this time, there were some golden nuggets for her to leverage. She could see the building blocks clearly, as though Willie had designed them specifically for her the past couple of months.

Once she determines where she wanted the company to go, she needs to make sure she has a leadership team in place who can create the roadmap to get there and be the ones driving it on a daily basis. She's going to need to think through her current circle of leadership, where the company needs to go, and if they are the right ones to get it there. First and foremost, she needs to turn her leadership circle into a leadership team. The C's rolled through her head: clarity, consistency, communication, collaboration, conflict, culture. She was only winning on the last C right now, so there was a lot of work to be done.

Pulling It All Together

Things to Know

- A misaligned team is easy to spot. There are tensions among the team, there are more gossip and personal agendas than problem solving, timelines and goals slip, blame and finger pointing are prevalent, and employee complaints and turnover are on the rise.

- Elements of team alignment — the C's:

  o **Clarity**: As CEOs, we provide the destination and determine who owns what part of the journey. It is their responsibility to then create the path.

  o **Consistency**: Keep the goals and messaging consistent. Any time we deviate or add, it can derail.

  o **Communication**: It needs to make sense, be two-way, have a common language, and be validated through a feedback loop.

  o **Collaboration**: Create a mission-critical case study to practice collaboration.

  o **Conflict**: Conflict a good thing for effective and aligned leadership teams. It can be easy to mistake disagreement for misalignment. Great leaders get that way from being surrounded by people with various strengths who can challenge thought processes, strategies, and plans.

  o **Culture**: "Culture eats strategy for breakfast." — Peter Drucker

Questions to Ask

- Are we building trust within our team?
- How are we doing, on a scale of 1–5, with each of the team alignment elements?

Next Step: Taking Action

Determine which of the team alignment elements would make the biggest impact if your company and leadership team worked on improving it.

Section 5: GET FORWARD MOVEMENT

Willie rejoined the group after a break for lunch. Before he could get the ball rolling, Logan raised his hand.

Logan sat back and very pointedly turned toward Carrie: "So Carrie, this is your third meeting with us. When you first introduced yourself, you seemed as though you were doing everything in your company, including washing the dishes at the end of the day. I can't imagine that is what you want to be doing for the next 10 years. We are here to push you and support you. What do you see as your role in the company going forward?"

Talk about being put on the spot! Carrie had given this a lot of thought. She did have a vision for the company. She enjoyed thinking about what it can be. She loved the idea of having a team of people who could support her vision, and that she could develop. She knew her communication needed improvement, but she was willing to put in the work.

Without hesitation, Carrie announced: "I am the company's single investor and the CEO. I'd like to not be managing everything on a daily basis and to spend more time developing additional channels of business. There is also a 'healthy children' project I have had in the back of my mind since I started the company. I want to bring people in my industry together to donate their time and food to teach children how to prepare healthy meals."

Logan paused, "Then this group is here to help remove any roadblocks that exist for you to get where you want to go."

CHAPTER 18

Remove the Roadblocks

Willie knew Carrie's No. 1 roadblock was herself. He wanted to expand on what removing the roadblocks would mean.

"The leadership of the organization needs to agree to make changes and operate differently," he said. "This includes the owner and/or CEO. Openly discuss what is driving the change and why it is needed. This discussion alone will help self-select those on the team who believe in the vision and direction of the company — and have a desire to do what is needed to achieve it. As much as we like to think anything is possible, expecting a different outcome without change doesn't work."

Willie shared a situation one of the COOs in his executive leadership roundtable had been through.

Mary was brought on as an interim COO by a CEO who had some big ideas and plans for the company. Once Mary started, she noticed that what the CEO referred to as the leadership team wasn't a leadership team. There's a difference between leaders and managers, and these were tactical, day-to-day managers who were operating the company but not leading it forward. They were not leading their business units; they were leading activities. The particular challenge of this assignment was the people who were managing (rather than leading) were forced to work this way, because the CEO didn't want them to actually lead.

While the CEO wanted the company turned around, he wanted full control of every decision and every point of the process. Mary had a tough conversation with the CEO. She asked if he was happy with the numbers and the current direction of the company. His response was easy: "No, Mary, that's why I brought you in." Mary continued: "The way it has been led is not going to take you to that level, even with me here. Are you open to being part of the answer?" Mary walked the CEO through her observations of the management team and a path to help them evolve into a leadership team, which included some changes in how he leads.

Willie reinforced the point: "If the company is not making the profits it wants to make, changes need to be made. Even with the right leadership team, without the support of the CEO, they aren't going to make it very far. The decision is binary: Are you going to embrace the change needed, or do you want to keep things the way they are?"

Raul, the attorney in the group, added that, as leaders, most of us have control issues. "Being aware of it is one thing, but managing it is a whole other situation," he said. "We need to be self-aware of our shortcomings and where we may be the possible roadblocks."

Self-Awareness

We need to have self-awareness, as we think through what we are good at and not so good at, and align them with what we enjoy doing. This includes how we interact with each other, our immediate teams, and the rest of the organization.

Raul, who is managing partner of his firm, shared a situation he had gone through. Due to some feedback and increased turnover, his firm came up with an initiative to have more kindness, but one of the managing partners was the antithesis of this with his aggressive behavior. It was trickling down, and the administrative staff was getting resentful. They don't want to be helpful when it gets to that point. They are happy to let the leaders fail. When administrative individuals understand how important they are, it goes a long way. Why would you stay late to help on something that isn't your direct responsibility if you don't feel what you do matters? They can get to the point of active sabotage if they get too resentful. This goes for everyone. The aggressive attorney was modeling the example for behavior in the firm.

Due to the increase in complaints and turnover, the human resources leader came up with the idea of a "kindness" initiative to influence their corporate culture. It wasn't going as smoothly as they'd hoped, so they brought in a coach who had a call with the partners. When the coach described some of the behaviors that were occurring, the aggressive partner modeling the behavior was completely unaware of where it was coming from. The coach walked through some of the symptoms of a dysfunctional leadership team. The aggressive partner's response was that they didn't have any of those issues. Another partner spoke up and said, "Yes, we do." The aggressive partner was shocked. Awareness is powerful. People in the organization pay very close attention to behavior. It's not what you say, but what you do.

Coaching your team on self-awareness and being authentic yourself will go a long way with your leadership team and toward removing some of the major roadblocks that can stall forward movement.

Carrie was reminded of the individual in her organization with similar behaviors. By not doing anything about it yet, she could see she was being the roadblock.

Getting and Giving Clarity

Evette knew all too well from being CEO of a turnaround that Carrie was going to need to be crystal clear about where her company was going and refocus the entire organization.

Evette shared: "In order to give clarity, we need to have clarity. When companies lose their way, it is often because they have lost focus. Clarity about where the company is going and how it will get there will help refocus the team and provide the much-needed energy and momentum to get there more quickly than it would have otherwise."

Be clear, concise, decisive, and conclusive. Once you have clarity as a leader, it gives your leadership team the destination and guardrails along the way to help the rest of the company get there.

Use a communication feedback loop, and ask questions rather than playing the telephone game. What did we say, what did we intend to say, what was heard, and what is being done as a result of it? Clarity and focus are such powerful tools, these are the first areas a new CEO will work on when stepping into an organization.

Evette shared from her turnaround experience: "The company was losing hundreds of thousands of dollars a month. To stay in business, they needed to become profitable quickly. They kept trying different things and ended up with 10 things they were counting on, when they really only had resources to do two things really well.

"First, I pulled everyone together, and we narrowed it down to the No. 1 priority we thought would make the biggest impact. I knew we needed to get motion and energy going with everyone pulling together. It is like a raft in the river. If someone is not rowing in the same direction, it will not end up well for the boat or the people in it. Once everyone was clear on where we were going and what each needed to do, we were able to execute and make a big impact."

CHAPTER 19

Comfort Zones

Willie reminded everyone of a past speaker who talked about challenging our teams' comfort zones.

Since our organizations are always in some type of transition, one of the roadblocks to getting forward momentum is a comfort-zone mindset. Staying within a comfort zone creates status quo rather than growth. A great quote from one of Willie's speakers was, "The hardest thing to do is stop doing things you know you shouldn't be doing."

Identifying what comfort zones exist in our organization, as well as who has the ability to go beyond the comfort zones and who doesn't, can help us remove this roadblock.

To help identify the extent to which our teams are willing to go beyond their comfort zones, the speaker suggested giving scenarios to them. It can be something as seemingly simple as, "We're thinking of changing the colors of our logo."

Greg told the group how impactful that speaker's message was for him: "The next time I want to test this out, I will say something like, 'I'm thinking about assigning parking spots.' As personal as I know parking can be, there is no way it would elicit the reaction I got when I suggested changing our logo colors. Wow! I am still recovering from that conversation. The responses ranged from, 'Why would we do that?' to 'I've been wanting to for years!' I sat back and watched the debate, who said what, who added to it, and their body language. Just like the speaker said, it was very telling about who was resistant to any type of change, who was ready to charge in gung-ho, and who sat back and watched while saying absolutely nothing. The goal was to identify who is stuck in their comfort zone and who can stretch beyond it. It was indicative of how they solve problems and address change. If they can't discuss and resolve something as basic as the color of the company logo or assigning parking spots, how are they going to be able to move the company forward?"

Carrie started to think of her own team and how that would go over. Since their logo hasn't been touched since the day she first designed it, she didn't think anyone would care. She'd have to pick something that was debatable, such as allowing the production team to choose what color hair nets they wanted to wear. She could see that debate going on for days.

CHAPTER 20

Let Your Leadership Team Lead

It had been a long day, but Willie could tell a lot of good had been accomplished. He ended the meeting with one parting thought: "Once you know you have the right team, they have clarity on where the company needs to go, they have the tools needed to get there, and you have removed the roadblocks, let them lead."

At the end of the meeting, Willie told Carrie she would be hosting and presenting in six months. She had experienced a few meetings and had a feel for what was expected. Willie challenged her to commit to doing things in her company differently before then.

Willie reminded her that she didn't need to do it all alone. Over the years, he has collected a great network of resources and people who can come in and help with any part of it. This would give her an outside perspective, likely speed up her progress, and supplement some of her gaps. She'd then decide what part of the support she wants longer term, and she'd have a good idea of those she wants to add to her team.

Carrie knew she would need some help. She could lean on the group to challenge her thoughts on where she wanted to go, but determining what needed to be done and having all the right people to create a roadmap was not how her brain worked. She definitely would be taking Willie up on his offer. For now, she was going to focus on where she wanted the company to go. It was time to start dreaming again!

Pulling It All Together

Things to Know

- We need to have self-awareness, as we think through what we are good at and not so good at, and align them with what we enjoy doing. It's not what you say but what you do.

- Leaders must be clear, concise, decisive, and conclusive.

- Once you know you have the right team, they have clarity on where the company needs to go, they have the tools needed to get there, and you have removed the roadblocks, let them lead.

Questions to Ask

- Am I going to embrace the change needed, or do I want to keep things the way they are?

- Do we have feedback loops for our communication? What did we say, what did we intend to say, what was heard, and what is being done as a result of it?

Next Step: Taking Action

- Identify what comfort zones exist in your organization, as well as who has the ability to go beyond their comfort zone and who doesn't.

- Identify where you and/or your team is getting stuck, and remove the roadblocks.

- Go dream, and let your team make the dream a reality!

Epilogue: This Founder's Journey

Six months later, it was Carrie's turn to host the group. Fortunately, her conference room was large enough to fit everyone. That meant the group could tour her facility and meet some of her team — her leadership team — before her presentation.

Where does Carrie want to take the company, and what does she want her role to be?

Carrie started off stating her name and title: "Hi, I'm Carrie, CEO of a growing food-manufacturing business. I plan to double the size of my business in the next 6 years.

"To do that, I have focused my efforts on those things I enjoy doing and am really good at. I have started a roundtable for leaders in my industry. That has resulted in some interesting opportunities for partnerships and possible acquisitions of smaller companies. Dividing my time into the following categories worked best for me to catch myself when I was working beyond or outside where I want to be:

- 50% of my time is spent on growth activities outside the company.
- 40% of my time is spent inside the company developing and aligning our team, especially as I bring in new individuals.

- 10% of my time is set aside for my aspirational projects, including the nonprofit I want to start."

What does Carrie need to accomplish to get there?

"I mentioned some possible smaller acquisitions. I worked with a business-growth consultant to help validate how I would double the size of my company in a realistic time frame of 6 years. There were a number of options, including international expansion. What aligned most with what I enjoy doing and where I want to spend my time was a combination of smaller acquisitions and organic growth expanding into new distribution channels.

"With the help of my part-time CFO, we did an annual forecast of how we will get there and the cash flow I'll need for each of those steps.

"Once I determined all that, I was able to identify what the milestones would be and what it would take to get there. Neither I nor anyone in my company has ever done an acquisition. Since the opportunities have started to find me rather than the other way around, I know I am going to need a formulated process for determining what makes sense for us.

"We are also going to need to figure out the production space, equipment, and talent we will need for each phase of this growth."

Whom does Carrie need to accomplish it?

"Dave is thriving. We talked through what he enjoyed doing and what role he wanted to play in the growth. He made a comment that brought me to tears. He said, 'Carrie, I was starting to wonder if you wanted to be running this company. It feels good to have you and your passion back.'

"I didn't realize I had lost myself. It was as though all of you reminded me of who I was and gave me a better framework to be the owner and CEO. I needed the nudge to run my business differently and the tools to do it. Dave is incredible at developing and inspiring our production teams. I didn't realize how many ideas everyone had for improving. Once I stopped attending all the meetings, people were more open with their suggestions. They felt as though speaking up about changing things I had created would have been disrespectful. Dave is taking his first vacation in two years. He is taking his wife to Niagara Falls. He doesn't know it yet, but I called and upgraded their hotel room. I realize I have appreciated his wife and all her support over the years almost as much as I have appreciated Dave.

"I have started to expose my food scientist SME, James, to more areas of the company, including client meetings. Our local university has executive extension courses. He has enrolled in a finance course, followed by an introductory leadership-development course. Depending on how he feels after those courses, I'm interviewing coaches to help create an individual on-the-job training plan for him.

"One of the toughest things was admitting the company had outgrown Karen. Karen enjoyed doing a little bit of everything and being the one to hold it together. As I started to formalize the direction, and make roles and expectations of those roles clear, Karen decided it wasn't somewhere she wanted to be. I gave her the time she needed to find something else. We had worked together for 10 years, and I really wanted what was best for her. Rather than directly replacing her, I brought in some additional administrative support with HR experience and a part-time HR consultant.

I needed someone to own the well-being of our employees, think about what they need next, and help me figure out what the company needs six months from now. So far, so good.

"I mentioned the part-time CFO, who is managing our accounting, giving me more insights on the financials, and working on some models of what it will look like to add the capacity we need. It has been a shift to go from knowing the numbers of the business off the top of my head to relying on someone else for them. It took some time to figure out what I needed to know on a daily, weekly, and monthly basis. I think we are in a good position with that until we get to the point of our first acquisition.

"Best of all, I just hired a full-time COO to run the daily operations of the business. Evette helped me identify an interim COO, Carlos, who helped me with a lot of this. I love Carlos, but he wasn't interested in coming on longer term, so he helped me figure out exactly what I need a COO to accomplish. Carlos is coaching me on the performance metrics for our new COO and holding me accountable to do regular check-ins to make sure the COO and I are on the same page.

"I am holding my first-ever strategic planning meeting. I have asked Willie to come in and help facilitate it. With all the shifts, we have some alignment to do, and I want to make sure everyone is clear on the direction I have for the company.

"Best of all, I have taken two vacations in the past six months. I was able to step away without worrying about what would happen if a fire broke out!"

Final Thought: Your Journey

The journey Carrie took isn't always as straight as it seems. I have been on this journey. I have helped others on this journey. Whether you are at the beginning, have been through it, or are somewhere in-between - I am here to support you in it and would love to hear your story.

Please contact me at: **findingleadership.co**

Acknowledgements

The book is dedicated to all the Carrie's who are brave and bold enough to start a business, to their teams dedicated to grow the business through each stage of its lifecycle, and to the Willie's who are there when needed to guide us all through it all. You have been my inspiration throughout.

Thank you to everyone who was open about their experiences, were genuine about how they felt, what they went through in their journey to either build the business or as part of the team to help build it.

I have such gratitude for all the owners and leadership who have let me into their companies over the years to share your challenges and let me be part of your journey.

About the Author

Kristen McAlister has spent most of her career helping companies create value and grow. She has spent the past 15 years teaching companies how to leverage leadership and build teams to support growth.

She is a speaker and multi-book author on topics including leadership teams, talent management, contingent workforce, and independent executive careers. Kristen is a mother, Ironman, and retired Marine wife.

www.ingramcontent.com/pod-product-compliance
Lightning Source LLC
Chambersburg PA
CBHW060616210326
41520CB00010B/1355